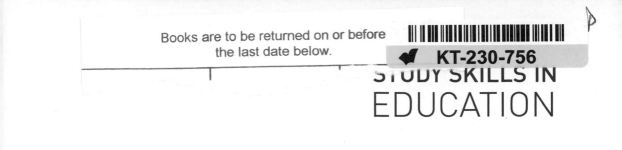
STUDY SKILLS IN
EDUCATION

Information
Skills for
Education
Students

STUDY SKILLS IN
EDUCATION

Information Skills for Education Students

Lloyd Richardson
and Heather McBryde-Wilding

LearningMatters

First published in 2009 by Learning Matters Ltd.

British Library Cataloguing in Publication Data
A CIP record for this book is available from the British Library.

ISBN: 978 1 84445 190 6

Cover and text design by Toucan Design
Project management by Swales & Willis Ltd, Exeter, Devon
Typeset by Swales & Willis Ltd, Exeter, Devon
Printed and bound in Great Britain by TJ International Ltd, Padstow, Cornwall

Learning Matters Ltd
33 Southernhay East
Exeter EX1 1NX
Tel: 01392 215560
info@learningmatters.co.uk
www.learningmatters.co.uk

FSC
Mixed Sources
Product group from well-managed
forests and other controlled sources
Cert no. SGS-COC-2482
www.fsc.org
© 1996 Forest Stewardship Council

Contents

1. Information skills in context

Education needs a new model of learning – learning that is based on the information resources of the real world . . .

(Breivik, 1998, p. 128)

Introduction

Changes in information and communications technology are radically transforming our lives and the pace of change is accelerating at such a rate that traditional patterns of education will no longer suffice if we are to cope with the economic and social challenges of the so-called Information Age. Consequently, the notions of *learning to learn* and *lifelong learning* have become accepted as essential elements of educational policy for the twenty-first century, not only in the United Kingdom, but throughout the developed world.

However, if you are to succeed as a self-directed and lifelong learner, you must not only have the skills that will enable you to make effective use of the information and communications technology that is available; you must also have the skills that will enable you to make effective use of the information that is available. These information skills are becoming increasingly important as information relentlessly encroaches upon virtually every aspect of our lives.

The purpose of this book is to help you to develop your information skills and, thereby, to become more information literate. The value of the book will depend on the extent to which you are self-motivated and prepared to engage with the reflective and practical tasks that feature in each of its main chapters. This does not mean that, having completed the tasks, you will become immune to *information anxiety*, but you should become better at finding and using the information that will you need in order to achieve your educational goals. In turn, as you develop these skills you will become more aware of and, therefore, able to avoid some of the pitfalls and false information trails that so often result in wasted time and effort.

Several excellent models have been proposed for the development of information skills at university level. These include: the American Library Association's *Information literacy competency standards for higher education*, the *Australian and New Zealand information literacy framework*, and the Society of College, National and University Librarian's *Seven headline skills* (SCONUL, 2003). The framework used in this book is a synthesis which draws upon each of these models, but reflects what the authors feel are the most important aspects of information literacy in light of their experience of working with education students across a wide range of courses. Thus, there are separate chapters on:

- recognising the need for information;

- information seeking strategies;

- locating and accessing information;

- evaluating information;

- presenting information in appropriate formats;

- self-assessment and self-reflection.

Although each chapter is self-explanatory, it is recommended that you initially work through them in sequence, rather than dipping in and out of the book. This is because information skills are, in a sense, hierarchical and if you are intent on developing your skills the best place to start is at the beginning. There is no quick and easy way to become more proficient at coping with the information demands that will be made on your course; you must be prepared to invest the necessary time and effort.

Information skills or information literacy?

The terms information skills and information literacy refer to the same thing, namely the ability to 'locate, access, evaluate, adapt and use information from a variety of sources to meet an information need' (Mackenzie et al., 2002). While this is not the only definition, or necessarily the best, it is a useful one since it concisely sums up what it means to be information literate. You are advised to compare it with some of the other definitions that are currently in use and to decide for yourself which one makes the most sense. Four very good alternatives can be found in *A short introduction to information literacy*. This document, which has been produced by the Chartered Institute of Library and Information Professionals (CILIP), can be accessed online by using any of the major search engines. All you need do is type in *CILIP* and the document's title.

The multiplicity of definitions (there are literally dozens) highlights one of the key challenges facing all students in higher education, which is being able to cope with information overload, that is, having so much information that you find it difficult to make a decision. This book should help you to rise to that challenge and, thereby, reduce your information load to more manageable proportions.

Despite the book's title, the terms *information skills* and *information literacy* are both used in the main body of the text. This reflects the fact that they are used interchangeably in much of the available literature on the subject and that they are in common use throughout the university sector, in the UK and abroad. (The term *information handling skills* is also sometimes used but it has not yet caught on to the same extent.) While some tutors and academic librarians prefer the term *information skills*, because they fear that students may resent being regarded as *information illiterates*, information literacy is more commonly used and, therefore, the term cannot be ignored (Webber and Johnston, 2006). Whatever the merits of this view, it is unhelpful as well as nonsensical to infer that any student in higher education is 'information illiterate', i.e. lacks the skills that are needed in order to locate, access, evaluate, adapt and use information. You already possess these skills and what really matters is how much further you may need to develop them.

The concept of information literacy is not new. Horton (2007, p.1) traces its roots back to the educational reform movements of the 1960s but makes clear that the idea did not originate in the work of any single author or research study. Rather it arose out of the convergence of many developments, including: a growing awareness amongst educationists that more emphasis should be placed on developing students' capacities for critical thinking and *learning how to learn*; the emergence of new forms of literacy, such as computer literacy and media literacy; the computer revolution and the opening up of the internet; and the advent of e-learning and distance learning technologies, which mean that post-compulsory education and training is increasingly taking place outside traditional institutional settings (ibid., p. 2).

Whether you choose to refer to this concept as *information literacy* or *information skills* is less important than understanding that it has no universally agreed definition and that, despite the computer revolution, information will continue to be available from many different sources and in many different formats. While you may be able to get through your course by relying primarily on information that you have downloaded from the internet, you are strongly advised not to become overly reliant upon electronic sources. That is, information skills involve much more than competence in the use of information technology and it is very unlikely that all of your course-related information needs will be satisfied by what you can find out online.

Information skills, study skills, and key skills

In order to set information skills in context it is helpful to consider some of the other skills initiatives that have been taken up by the university sector. As you are probably aware, all universities and colleges of higher education offer students help with the development of *skills*, but the pattern of provision is complex. For example, some elements of skills development are likely to be embedded directly into your course curriculum, while others may take the form of additional modules or programmes. Help with skills development will also be available from some of the non-academic staff who provide your institution's support services.

A confusing variety of names is used to describe these skills, consequently what one university calls study skills another may refer to as learning skills, or academic skills. Since these are the skills that you will need in order to study effectively they include being able to locate, access, evaluate, adapt and use information. In other words, there is much common ground between study skills and information skills.

Similarly, the terms graduate skills, generic skills and transferable skills are all used to describe the attributes that are supposed to distinguish the abilities of graduates from those who have not gone on to higher education. The picture is further complicated because there is no definitive list of graduate skills (i.e. individual universities identify different sets of skills) and some graduate skills, such as *competence in oral and written communication* and *competence in the use of information technology* are also considered to be study skills.

In addition, there are key skills (or core skills) and these have been central to the policy debates over post-compulsory education since the late 1970s. Exactly what these skills are and how they should be defined has been the subject of much controversy and the issue may not yet be resolved, despite the advent of the new Key Skills Award.

The Dearing report (1997) recommended that the development and assessment of key skills should be integrated into all undergraduate programmes; and identified these skills as oral and written communication, numeracy, the use of communications and information technology, and learning how to learn. They were described as being *key* to the future success of all graduates, whatever they may decide to do after university.

Four years later the Qualifications and Curriculum Authority came up with an alternative list of six skills which it concluded were essential for success in education (including higher education), work, and life in general (QCA, 2001). These are the application of number, communication, improving own learning and performance, information and communication technology, problem solving, and working with others. The first three of these are referred to as the main key skills and the latter three as the wider key skills. Together they form the basis of the Key Skills Award and earn UCAS points for university applicants.

Some universities have adopted these six key skills as their generic (or graduate) skills while the Open University has gone a step further and added information literacy to the list of key skills on its LearningSpace website (Open University, 2008). This does not mean that other universities and colleges have failed to recognise the importance of information skills but that, unlike Australia, for example, the UK does not yet have an 'overarching cohesive strategy to information skills training in higher education' (MMU, 2007, p. 5). Ideally information skills, like the other key skills, will become integrated into all higher education course curricula, as the SCONUL task force has recommended (SCONUL, 2003).

Thus it can be seen that although the terms information skills, study skills and key skills refer to three distinct sets of skills, and however imprecisely they may be defined, these sets of skills overlap. That information skills have not received the same level of attention that has been accorded to study skills and key skills does not indicate that they are any less important. Rather, it shows instead that the UK's higher education sector has a long way to go before it catches up with its counterparts in Australia, New Zealand and the United States.

Information skills and information technology skills

Information skills are mainly (but not entirely) cognitive skills, so it would be wrong to assume that just by becoming more adept at using information technology that you will also become more information literate. For example, in the case of a coursework assignment, before you begin to search for information you must first read the assignment brief and *think* about what you have been asked to do and the information that you will need in order to do it. The same applies when you are evaluating and synthesising information, as the relevant chapters in this book will make clear. In other words, you must think critically in order to make effective use of the information that you find and such thinking is entirely unrelated to your level of technological competence.

That does not mean that good word processing and network application skills are unimportant. On the contrary, they are invaluable when it comes to finding and presenting information, and such competence may even be an assessed component of your course. Further, you would be seriously disadvantaged if you were unable to access electronically formatted sources of information. However, the underlying purpose of any course-related task in higher education is likely to take you beyond the acquisition of knowledge (i.e. information) and require you to demonstrate your *understanding*. In order to do this you do not need good computer skills; you need good thinking skills.

Thus, while information technology skills and information skills are interrelated (like study skills and key skills) they are not one and the same thing. The essence of this distinction can be easily illustrated by pointing out that information skills are primarily about information, and information technology skills are primarily about technology.

The significance of information skills for education students

If you are already working in education or intend to do so in any capacity, from a pre-school setting to university level, you will be expected to engage in lifelong learning, i.e. to continue updating your knowledge and skills throughout your working life. This may require a little clarification since the term lifelong learning is, like information literacy itself, interpreted in different ways. Here it is used to describe any intentional learning in which you participate, whether it is delivered formally or self-managed.

Since information skills are an essential element of lifelong learning (Bundy et al., 2004, p. 1) you will need to develop these skills further, especially if you are determined to assume more responsibility for your own learning. The real value in taking this step is that it will lead to greater personal autonomy, that is, it will make you better informed and, thereby, less dependent upon the thinking of others. In order to be a good educational practitioner you must have confidence in your powers of judgement and your ability to deal with work-related problems. This means being able to find the right information and evaluate it, so that you can arrive at your own conclusions and make your own informed decisions. The alternative is to opt for pre-digested information and defer to other people's opinions on important educational issues rather than working out your own. This may be acceptable in the short term but it is not advisable as a long-term strategy.

One educational issue which is very controversial is that of learning styles. Although teachers are encouraged to believe that a thorough knowledge of their pupils' individual learning preferences will lead to better lesson planning, increased motivation and higher levels of achievement, there is very little reliable and valid research evidence to support the idea that responding to learning styles has much influence on learning (Coffield et al., 2004, p. 2). It is surprising that so many people who are working in education seem to have readily accepted the claims made by those who market learning styles inventories, when the case for them is far from proven. The point here is not to enter into the learning styles debate but to use it to demonstrate that the study of education, like any other academic discipline, will lead you into areas of controversy. When it does, you should not be afraid to take a stand, especially if the controversy relates to your own area of expertise and you are well informed. This is another way of saying that educational *experts* are not always right. If they were, there would be no controversies; the arguments would all be resolved and consensus would prevail.

A word of advice is offered about the implications of doing more of your own thinking. Even though it is no longer permissible to burn heretics, there are other ways of punishing them. Education has its own orthodoxies and some tutors may resent the expression of unorthodox opinions, however compelling the evidence that is offered in support of them. Therefore you should remember who is marking your work and accept that sometimes there can be a fine line between offering a rigorous defence of your own point of view and appearing to be opinionated. This does not mean that you should be afraid to say what you think but that you should get in the habit of *thinking* carefully about how you say it.

Your time in higher education should give you the opportunity to do some careful thinking and to further develop your information skills; the two go together. If you are to take full advantage of this opportunity you must acquire the competence that will enable you to use all of the information resources that your institution makes available, for self-managed as well as formal learning. A good place to begin this process is by assessing your current level of skills competence to identify your strengths and weaknesses.

Self-assessment task

There is no standardised information skills test for education students at British universities and this task is not intended as a substitute. The questions relate directly to the learning outcomes in the main chapters of the book and you must be candid about your ability if the task is to serve any practical purpose. What matters is not your current level of information skills competence but the extent to which you are prepared to take responsibility for developing it.

Since students tend to over or under estimate their abilities when they are asked to self-assess, you are advised to think carefully before answering each question. Effective self-assessment requires a degree of self-reflection, so you should not rush through the task.

1. Recognising the need for information

Defining your needs

When you have been set a task (e.g. an essay) how confident are you in your ability to interpret the assignment brief in order to decide what information you need and where to look for it?

Determining the value and relevance of potential sources

You will usually have to choose from a wide variety of printed and electronic sources, depending on the type of assignment. How good are you at narrowing down your choice to those sources that will provide the most useful information?

Constraints that may affect your search

Information searches are constrained by such factors as time, cost and ease of access. Do you deal with these constraints effectively (e.g. do you manage your time efficiently when you are looking for information)?

2. Information seeking strategies

Selecting appropriate methods to find information

Your selection will depend on the task in which you are engaged and you may have to use more than one method (e.g. library and internet searching, interviews, and observations). Do you find it easy to choose the most appropriate information search methods?

Formulating and executing a search strategy

A well-planned search is more likely to succeed than one that is poorly planned. How good are you at planning information searches?

Using appropriate methods to find information

Selecting an appropriate search method is one thing, using it is another. How competent are you when you are searching for information, in a library and online?

3. Locating and accessing information

The range of sources

The range of education-related information sources can seem overwhelming. Do you think that you have a good understanding of these sources and how to locate them?

Searching effectively

The purpose of any search is to find the information that you need in order to carry out a task. Do you think that you do this effectively?

4. Evaluating information

Assessing the usefulness and significance of information

You should evaluate every information source that you intend to use. Are you aware of the evaluation criteria that can be applied to assess printed, electronic and oral sources of information and, if you are, do you apply them effectively?

Using information from different sources to create a synthesis

For most assignments you will be expected to use the main ideas that you find in your sources to create your own new interpretation or argument. This is known as creating a synthesis. Do you think that you are good at it?

5. Presenting information in appropriate formats

Presenting work in appropriate formats

Different types of assignment (e.g. essays and reports) are formatted in different ways. How confident are you when using these different formats?

Understanding the stylistic conventions that apply to academic writing

You will have to observe the common stylistic conventions that apply to academic writing. How familiar are you with these conventions?

The ethical use of information

You must comply with your institution's policies on confidentiality and plagiarism, as well as copyright law. Do you feel that you are sufficiently aware of these requirements and that you know to use information ethically?

Follow-up assessment

There is a more detailed self-assessment task in Chapter 7, which addresses the wider range of information skills and sub-skills that are the focus of this book. However, neither assessment task is intended as a means of determining whether or not you have achieved a satisfactory level of information literacy. In a constantly changing information environment this is probably not possible. Rather, in the context of further developing your information skills competence, you should regard the assessment tasks as starting points.

Summary of key points

In order to succeed as a self-directed and lifelong learner you must not only have the skills that will enable you to make effective use of information and communications technology, you must also have the skills that will enable you to make effective use of information itself.

Despite the computer revolution, information will continue to be available from many different sources and in many different formats. Thus, you should not become overly reliant upon electronic sources of information (e.g. assume that all of your information needs can be satisfied by what you can find out online).

Developing your information skills will not only help you to become better informed, it will also make you less dependent upon the thinking of others and, thereby, give you greater confidence in your own powers of judgement and your ability to deal with work-related problems.

References and further reading

The following sources offer invaluable insights into the origins and development of the concept of information literacy, and its significance within the context of lifelong learning.

Breivik, P.S. (1998) *Student learning in the information age.* Phoenix: Oryx Press.

Bundy, A. (ed.) (2004) *Australian and New Zealand Information literacy framework: principles, standards and practices.* 2nd edition. Adelaide: Australian and New Zealand Institute for Information Literacy [online] Available at: **www.anziil.org/ resources/Info%20lit%202nd%20edition.pdf** While this document is intended for university staff, the framework itself (in the words of its authors) *provides a structure for students to have an awareness and understanding of their interaction with information.* It also presents a brief chronology of the development of information literacy initiatives in Australia and New Zealand.

CILIP (2007) *A short introduction to information literacy.* London: Chartered Institute of Library and Information Professionals. [online] Available at: **www.cilip.org.uk/ policyadvocacy/learning/informationliteracy/definition/introduction.htm** This brief document (i.e. it is only two A4 sides of text) is easy to access and read. You are strongly advised to have a look at it.

Coffield, F. et al. (2004) *Should we be using learning styles?: what research has to say to practice.* London: Learning and Skills Research Centre. [online] Available at: **www.lsneducation.org.uk/pubs/pages/041540.aspx** This report offers an illuminating insight into the complexities and uncertainties that surround the debate on learning styles.

Dearing, R. (1997) (chairman) *Higher education in the learning society: Report of the National Committee of Inquiry into higher education.* London: HMSO. [online] Available at: **www.leeds.ac.uk/educol/ncihe/**

Horton, F.W. (2008) *Understanding information literacy: a primer.* Paris: Unesco. [online] Available at: **unesdoc.unesco.org/images/0015/001570/157020e.pdf** This document offers an *easy-to-read, non-technical overview explaining what information literacy means* and although it is aimed at policy makers and other professionals, it should also be of interest to anyone who is interested in finding out more about information literacy.

Iannuzzi, P. et al. (2000) *Information literacy competency standards for higher education.* Chicago: American Library Association [online] Available at: **www.ala.org/acrl/ilcomstan.html**

Mackenzie, A. et al. (2002) *The Big Blue: information skills for students, final report.* [online] Available at: **www.leeds.ac.uk/bigblue/finalreport.html**

MMU Library (2007) *The Big Blue: literature review: the UK position.* Manchester: Manchester Metropolitan University [online] Available at: **www.library.mmu.ac.uk/bigblue/litreviewuk** While this document is also intended for university staff rather than students, its discussion of information skills developments within the higher education sector is well worth reading.

Open University (2008) *1 Introduction to key skills.* [online] Available at: www.openlearn.open.ac.uk/mod/resource/view.php?id=188594

QCA (2001) *Key skills update September 2001.* [online] Available at: www.qca.org.uk/qca_7011.aspx

SCONUL (2003) *Information skills in higher education: a SCONUL position paper.* London: Society of College, National and University Libraries. [online] Available at: www.sconul.ac.uk/groups/information_literacy/papers/Seven_pillars.html In addition to explaining what information skills are and why they are important, the SCONUL team also discuss the information skills model that they have devised.

Webber, S. and Johnston, B. (2006) *Information literacy: definitions and models.* [online] Available at: www.dis.shef.ac.uk/literacy/definitiions.htm The title of this web page is self-explanatory and its authors have done a good job of collating and comparing a range of definitions and models of information literacy.

2. Recognising the need for information

Information literate students recognise when information is required and can identify the nature and extent of their information needs in a range of contexts.

Learning outcomes

Having worked through this chapter you should be better able to:

- define your information needs in response to a variety of course-related activities (e.g. when planning and writing essays, preparing for school placements, and revising for examinations);

- determine the value and relevance of potential information sources (printed, electronic and oral) which can be used to address your information needs;

- identify any significant constraints of time, cost and access which may make particular information sources less worthwhile than others;

- critically examine the sources that you have selected, to further clarify or reassess your information needs.

The information dilemma

As a student you will be confronted by a bewildering volume and variety of information sources, i.e. *choices*. There will also be an expectation on the part of your tutors that you will be able to locate, access and evaluate these sources, so as to ensure that the work you produce (including your contributions to seminar groups and class discussions) is underpinned by a selection of balanced, authoritative, and up to date information. This information dilemma extends beyond the demands of higher education and impinges upon many aspects of social and working life. Further, competence in information skills is regarded as an essential ´prerequisite for participative citizenship and social inclusion´ (Bundy, 2004, p. 4). Even so, the skills that will enable you to satisfy your general information needs, in an information abundant world, are essentially the same as those that are required to achieve success at college or university. However, if you are to satisfy your needs you must understand that having a large quantity of information does not, of itself, make you better informed. What really matters is your ability to be critical and skilful when it comes to selecting from and using the information that you have found, in order to achieve your desired goals.

Information failure

A frequent criticism that tutors make of students' work is to highlight their failure to present *both sides of the argument* or to consider *alternative points of view.* Another fault that characterises many failed essays and reports is that students arrive at conclusions or make inferences which have *insufficient evidence* to support them. In other words, students sometimes lose marks because their assignments are based upon inadequate information. This inadequacy can be qualitative as well as quantitative. That is, work can be marked down not only because students do not draw upon a sufficient range of sources in constructing their arguments, but also because they rely too heavily upon authors who lack authority in the topic that is being debated, or they use sources that are out of date. Since new electronic methods make information retrieval easier than ever before, some tutors regard such failures as inexcusable.

These problems are less likely to arise where assignment briefs are accompanied by *recommended reading lists*, but this is not always the case. For example, when tackling the literature review for a dissertation or other investigative study, you will almost certainly be expected to *define your own information needs*. So it would be wrong to assume that you can always rely upon someone else to tell you what you need to know and where you can find it.

Defining your information needs

Assuming that your most pressing information needs will relate to your coursework, rather than your social life, how you go about defining them should be determined by the assignments that you are set. Information needs are always task-specific. That is, the nature and quantity of the information that you require will depend on the task you are undertaking. If, for instance, you are evaluating a school placement it may be appropriate to make use of oral sources (such as interviews with staff) or samples of pupils' handwriting; but in most cases the information that you are likely to need will be available in printed and electronic formats.

When it comes to choosing between oral, printed and electronic sources your choice should be guided by the specific demands of the task and a consideration of which of the three main types of source will yield the information that you are after. You should also be aware of the expectations of your tutors, e.g. some may prefer that you use a combination of printed and electronic sources when it comes to essay and report writing.

Oral sources

Interviews are sometimes a good way of obtaining information for a report or dissertation but they require careful preparation and can be very time-consuming. They may be formal or informal but do not confuse them with *having a chat*; they are an important method of data (i.e. *information*) gathering.

Lectures can also yield valuable information, especially if they are delivered by speakers of note, but if you rely too heavily on them (e.g. in writing an essay) your tutors may be unimpressed with your apparent reluctance to make use of a wider range of information sources.

Radio and television broadcasts (which, if recorded, are really electronic sources) can also provide useful information but it pays to be selective. You may end up listening to a one-hour programme to obtain a one-line quotation, and that would be a poor return for the time that you had invested.

Printed sources

The quickest way to gain an impression of the range of printed sources that are available to you is to have a look around the education section of your institution's library. Amongst the most important of these will be books, journals and government publications (e.g. texts concerned with the National Curriculum, copies of Education Acts and official reports), some of which will also be available online.

If you find out which of these sources can also be downloaded, it will spare you unnecessary trips to the library and leave you with more time for thinking, reading and writing.

Electronic sources

As with printed texts, you should take time to visit your library to find out what is on offer, and how to access those electronic sources that will provide you with the course-related information that you are likely to need. Your tutors may expect you to use e-books and e-journals, or to demonstrate your internet search competence in some other way, and it would be in your interests not to disappoint them.

Begin the process of defining your information needs by deciding exactly what it is that you need to find out, and why. This saves time by enabling you to identify and eliminate less relevant sources, thereby allowing you to focus on those that really matter.

Initial decisions about the nature and quantity of the information that you require should only be taken when you *know* what it is that you are expected to do (e.g. when you have a clear understanding of the assignment brief). If you are unsure, do not guess; if you do, you may get it wrong and lose marks. Some tutors write assignment briefs that are as confusing as the work that their students produce in response to them. Asking tutors to make things clearer is sometimes necessary and it can spare you a great deal of wasted effort and disappointment.

Practical task

Defining your information needs

Make a *brief* list of what you think your information needs would be in order to carry out the following task.

> *For pupils whose attainments fall significantly below the expected levels at a particular key stage, a much greater degree of differentiation will be necessary.*
> (QCA, 2008)

You are required to prepare and deliver a 10-minute oral presentation on the implications of this statement for classroom teachers. You may focus on a subject and key stage of your choice.

The activity relates directly to the first of the three principles for inclusion which underpin the National Curriculum, so you may already be familiar with them.

When you have completed your list please read the comments below.

There can, of course, be no definitive list since information needs will vary greatly between individuals, although you may have decided that it would be helpful to find out:

* which QCA document the quotation is taken from in order to gain a greater sense of context;

* what the expected attainment levels are for your chosen key stage and subject;

* more about what is meant by *attainments that fall significantly below* and *a much greater degree of differentiation* (presentations have audiences and you could be asked some difficult questions);

* where you can find some examples of curricular differentiation to illustrate the points that you intend to make in your presentation.

On a more practical note, you may want to familiarise yourself with the room in which you will deliver your presentation and any equipment that you intend to use. (I saw a student have a disaster because the university's software could not open the PowerPoint presentation on her memory stick; if only she had taken the time to find this out beforehand, this would not have happened.)

It would also help to know the size of your audience if you are expected to provide handouts and if you are uneasy about delivering presentations (many students are) you may want to consult some of the relevant study skills resources that are available in your institution's library, or online. These can provide invaluable advice (i.e. information) on planning and delivering presentations, and are frequently overlooked by students who do not recognise that their information needs often extend well beyond the acquisition of facts and figures.

The important thing is not the extent to which your list compares with mine but the extent to which it reflects your information needs in relation to the task that has been set. The only person who can define these needs is you, and this means taking the time to *think* about them first, so that you have a good idea of what it is you *need* to look for, before you start looking.

Determining the value and relevance of potential information sources

You will not be able to consult every relevant source of information, nor will your tutors expect you to do so. There will be too many of them and if you spend too long tracking down and pondering over books, journals and websites, you will have insufficient time left in which to complete your assignment to the required standard before the submission deadline. The knack lies in acquiring the skills which enable you to identify sufficient authoritative sources to meet your information needs, as quickly as possible.

In other words, time itself is a valuable resource and it must be used wisely.

Thus (to borrow a term used in the world of finance) you should try to become more information-efficient. This means learning how to make the most out of a chosen selection of information sources, rather than trying to find out *everything* there is to know and becoming weighed down by the sheer volume of information that you have identified.

You will get better at doing this through a combination of practice and self-critical reflection. A good place to start is by clarifying your thoughts on exactly what it is that gives some sources *authority*, i.e. makes them more reliable than others.

(Reflective task)

Determining the value and relevance of information sources

Consider *what*, in your opinion, makes a source of information reliable (i.e. makes it one which you might choose to consult rather than ignore). Compare your ideas with the comments made below.

In the case of information that is in print or electronically available, your tutors would probably concur that you should normally draw upon sources that are: accurate, up to date, relatively unbiased, and the work of people who are acknowledged to have expertise in the subject. I say *normally* because there can be good reasons for using out of date or biased sources if you are, for example, tracing the historical development of educational policy or discussing gender inequality in schooling.

In addition, you will almost certainly find that most of the sources included on your reading lists have extensive bibliographies (i.e. the authors tell you where they got their information), are from reputable publishers, and are based on sound research or first-hand experience.

If you confine your choice of printed and electronic sources to the work of those who have acknowledged expertise it is more likely that they will be accurate and unbiased. Educational *experts* do not want to risk having their books, journal articles or research reports held up to ridicule by their peers. The same applies to oral sources, although it may be harder to satisfy yourself about their accuracy and lack of bias, since they will not be subject to the same kind of public scrutiny as those which get into print.

Identifying any significant constraints of time, cost and access which may make particular sources of information less worthwhile than others

In their booklet *Information literacy standards for higher education*, Iannuzzi et al. (2000, p. 8) describe the information literate student as one who weighs up the costs and benefits of acquiring the needed information by finding out how readily available it is and then deciding upon a realistic plan and timeline in which to acquire it. The key words here are *considers* and *realistic*.

That is, before you leap into action and start searching for information, you should consider the time and effort that it may involve (i.e. you should be information-efficient). You should also be realistic about what you can expect to achieve in the time that is available.

Similar advice is offered by the Chartered Institute of Library and Information Professionals (CILIP, 2007), who recommend that any decision about the use of an information source should be tempered by the ease and speed with which it can be located and accessed. This in turn requires an understanding of the merits of individual resource types (printed, electronic and oral) and when it is appropriate to make use of them (ibid.).

Such decision-making is part of what being in higher education is all about. You may decide that it is better to buy an important book so that you have your own copy, rather than have it on temporary loan. While sometimes you can quickly obtain all of the information that you need from online sources, on other occasions it may take longer because you decide to request an inter-library loan or visit another library. These are choices that you have to make.

Colleges and universities offer help to students who wish to develop their information finding skills; do not hesitate to seek such help when you need it.

Unless you familiarise yourself with the various information sources (i.e. resources) that your institution makes available, and find out how to access them, it is unlikely that you will be able to make informed choices when it comes to deciding which are worth using and which are not.

Practical task

Identifying and accessing electronic sources of information

Identify which education-related electronic sources of information are provided by your institution, and find out how to access them.

This will take time and may require a combination of: checking out the appropriate rooms, reading any relevant institutional literature, talking to library and IT staff, and trying out the hardware and software.

The effort that you put into this will pay dividends in the longer term. If you do not do it, you may leave yourself cut off from many of the educational publications that are now available online.

Critically examining your sources to further clarify your information needs

It is sometimes necessary to re-evaluate the nature and extent of our information needs in light of our initial search results (Bundy, 2004, p.12). In other words, we do not always find everything that we want first time round, so that there is still an information gap to fill; while some of what we do find provides us with new insights into the topic that we are investigating and makes us decide to change the focus of our search.

However, while it often pays to reconsider your information needs as you examine some of the sources that you have selected and find out more about the topic, you should also heed the warning given by Bell (2005, p. 89), who states that:

> literature searching and particularly computer searching can become compulsive and easily overlap into the time allocated for other essential tasks, so at some stage you have to tell yourself that 'Enough is enough'.

In order to resist this compulsion and avoid wasting time, you must not lose sight of the purpose of your search, which is to enable you to find sufficient information to successfully complete a specific task. Thus, the point at which you reach the stage where you decide that *enough is enough*, will depend on what you are doing. If the assignment comes with a recommended reading list the decision should be relatively straightforward, while in the case of a dissertation you may find it far more challenging. Nonetheless, your tutors will expect you to exercise your own critical judgement when assessing and re-assessing your information needs, whatever the task that you have been set.

An illustration of how you might further clarify or reassess your information needs in relation to an essay task is included, as the final step, in the worked example that follows.

Worked example

Recognising when information is required and identifying the nature and extent of your information needs in relation to a specific task

This example is intended to demonstrate how you might go about identifying your information needs in relation to an essay task. There is no single *right* way of doing this, not least because, as with any assignment there will be differences in how individual students interpret the task and, therefore, differences in how they decide to approach it.

The task

In an essay of 2000 words, critically discuss the issue of boys' underachievement in secondary education. Identify the underlying causes and consider what schools can do to address them.

1. Understanding the task in order to define your information needs

Critical discussion means *examining by argument* so you must find some evidence of boys' underachievement to examine. In a 2000 word essay you will not be able to engage in a detailed debate; instead, you would probably be expected to present an overview of the nature and extent of the problem, its main causes, and any significant steps that schools can take to deal with them.

2. Determining the value and relevance of potential information sources

Unless you are drawing upon a lecture or broadcast by an *expert*, you should confine your search to printed and electronic sources.

Your institution's library should have some published material on boys' under-achievement and it would be helpful to examine these sources, in order to decide which are the most up to date and authoritative (i.e. worth using), and why.

Since the performance of schools is regularly monitored, a good place to start looking for electronic sources is *The standards site* (the website of the Department for Children, Schools and Families). This includes a *Gender and achievement* site with a *Case studies and research section* as well as a list of *Published titles*, which together contain a wealth of relevant information.

3. Identifying any significant constraints which may affect your choice of sources

If you are a part-time student living miles from your university, access to the library may be limited; and if you travel in on a day off work, your library visit could be expensive and time consuming. Thus, you may opt for electronic sources. This should not matter (there are plenty of them) provided that you find the information that you require and use it effectively to complete the task.

On the other hand, if you are a full-time student living on campus, you may be able to spend hours in the library scrutinising texts and reflecting upon your information needs. However, this does not necessarily mean that you will produce a better essay.

4. Critically examining your sources to further clarify your information needs

The research reports included on the *Gender and achievement* site reveal a complex pattern of boys' underachievement across the curriculum, and indicate that social class and ethnicity are much more significant factors than gender. They also identify five underlying causes of boys' underachievement and five strategies which schools can adopt to address them.

At this point you may decide that you have enough information on *causes and strategies*, but that you would like to find out more about the apparent causes of boys' performance in particular subjects and the relative significance of social class and ethnicity, to illustrate the complexity of the issue in your discussion.

Thus, you would have to reassess your needs and consider other potential sources of information, as well as any constraints which may affect your choice. Provided that your information search continues to be guided by a clear understanding of what it is that you are trying to find out and why, you should not have too much trouble in deciding when *enough is enough*, and that the time has come to stop looking for information and to start using it.

Summary of key points

Information needs are always task-specific, so that your choice of oral, printed or electronic sources must be guided by the demands of the task in which you are engaged and a consideration of which of these sources is most likely to provide the information that you require.

To define your information needs you must first decide what it is that you wish to find out and why. This saves time by enabling you to identify and eliminate less relevant sources, thereby allowing you to focus on those that really matter.

Limit your choice of information sources to those that are up to date, authoritative, and which you can access without any significant constraints of time, cost and effort.

Higher education institutions offer help to students who wish to develop their information skills; do not hesitate to seek such help if you need it.

It pays to familiarise yourself with the various information sources that your institution makes available and to find out how to access them.

Having access to a large quantity of information does not, of itself, make you better informed. What really matters is your ability to be a critical and skilful user of information, in order to achieve your desired goals.

References and further reading

There is an extraordinary amount of *information* on information skills, much of which is available online. Depending on your own information needs, you may wish to consult some of the sources which are listed below.

Bell. J. (2005) *Doing your research project: a guide for first-time researchers in education, health and social science.* 4th edition. Maidenhead: Open University Press. This is an excellent beginners' guide to educational research, with easy to follow advice on how to manage information and how to use libraries effectively. There is probably a copy in your own institution's library.

Bundy, A. (ed.) (2004) *Australian and New Zealand information literacy framework: principles, standards and practices.* 2nd edition. Adelaide: Australian and New Zealand Institute for Information Literacy. [online] Available at: **www.anziil.org/ resources/Info%20lit%202nd%20edition.pdf** This text is aimed at academic librarians but also *provides a structure for students to have awareness and understanding of their interaction with information.*

CILIP (2007) *Information literacy: the skills.* London: Chartered Institute of Library and Information Professionals. [online] Available at: **www.cilip.org.uk/policy advocacy/learning/informationliteracy/definition/skills.htm?cssversion=printable** The Cilip website includes a useful section on freedom of information.

Department for Children, Schools and Families (2008) *The standards site.* [online] Available at: **www.standards.dfes.gov.uk/** This site provides direct links to a wealth of information on education.

Iannuzzi, P. et al. (2000) *Information literacy competency standards for higher education.* Chicago: American Library Association. [online] Available at: **www.ala.org/acrl/ilcomstan.html** This document discusses how higher education providers can help their students to develop information literacy skills, through a cross-curricular approach.

QCA (2008) *National curriculum statutory inclusion statement.* London: Qualifications and Curriculum Authority. [online] Available at: **http://curriculum.qca.org.uk/ key-stages-3-and-4/organising-your-curriculum/inclusion/statutory_ inclusion_statement/index.aspx**

3. Information seeking strategies

Information literate students are able to access information both effectively and efficiently for any given need.

Learning outcomes

Having worked through this chapter you should be better able to:

- determine which tools are the most applicable for any information gathering activity;

- formulate and execute search strategies that are appropriate for any given topic, and for the tools you are using;

- use appropriate methods to obtain information and understand how to select relevant and authoritative sources;

- maintain an up to date knowledge of information technology and tools, and the sources and methods required to use these effectively.

What tools should you use?

The amount of information available to us in the Information Age is increasing at a phenomenal rate and it is often difficult to know when different types of information should be used, and which ones will be the most useful for any given circumstance.

If you are to develop a convincing argument you will need to ensure that you choose a variety of sources of information that give different viewpoints on a topic, as well as providing support to the ideas that you have. Do not make the mistake of placing too much reliance on one source of information. Expect to use both printed and human sources, as well as the electronic ones, because for certain topics they can be a valuable information source.

The best starting point, when researching a topic for an assignment, is to use the high quality resources available through your library. For example subject specific databases of journal references will usually give you much more relevant, good quality and specific information than internet search engines. This is because the internet has plenty of poor quality, out of date or biased information on it, as well as the good, so be careful not to be too dependent on it as a source. You can increase your chances of finding high quality information on the web by using academic gateways and portals, which we will discuss later.

An outline of research tools

The type of assignment you are preparing and its topic will play a large part in determining which types of information you need. It also influences which tools you will need to use to find your information. The most important thing to think about when using any research tool is how useful it will be to you in relation to what you are trying to find. Ask yourself if it is reliable, and hence accurate, if it is easy for you to use, and whether you can access it (you might need a password, etc.). You should also find out whether you will have to use it in a certain physical location, whether it will give you everything you need, or whether you will need to use other resources as well.

Reflective task

Which research tools can I search to find information?

Think about research tools you may have used already to search for information, such as the internet. Ask yourself how effective they were for finding what you wanted. Compare your thoughts with the information provided below.

There is a wide range of research tools available to students, but how do you know which ones you might need to use to carry out your research? In addition what do you need to know about them, are there any tips to ensure you use them effectively and what exactly do they offer access to?

Library catalogues – the online catalogues of libraries allow you to find out what a library holds. You can usually search them to find details of books, reports, journal titles and other materials. Start with your own library catalogue to identify material that is more likely to be readily available to you.

What search techniques can you use on the library catalogue? Firstly if there is something specific you want to find, do simple searches using title, author or subject/keyword fields.

The library classification scheme can help you find other relevant books because books are classified by the subject that they cover rather than their title, and so books about the same topic are shelved together. Use the shelf marks you find from your initial search, as a search itself. This allows you to replicate the act of browsing the shelves, but will be more effective because the catalogue will show details of items the library holds, even if they are on loan at the time.

If the catalogue uses subject headings then look at those used for any items you have already found and try a search with these headings to see all the items that use the same headings. Online catalogues with hyperlinks make searching like this so much easier for you.

Indexes and abstracts – these allow you to search across the contents of a wide range of journal titles for articles that have been written about a particular topic or by certain authors. They can cover quite specific subject areas, or be very general in nature and although there are still a few that are paper based, most indexes and abstracts come in the form of electronic databases. Some of the electronic databases also include references to chapters in books, theses and conference papers, and some allow you to search for articles that cite another author's work.

Indexes generally just give you the reference to the item, with little indication of the actual content, whereas abstracting databases include a synopsis of the item to help you find out about it before reading the whole thing; and often this is written by the author of the item.

Most of the electronic databases you encounter will be using the internet as a platform and you should not confuse this with searching the internet itself.

Many databases are subscription based, so will only be available to you if your institution pays for access, and you may need a specific login to use them, especially if you are working off-site. The library web pages of your institution may list the databases they subscribe to and include more useful information about what subject coverage they offer and how to use them effectively.

An example of a relevant indexing database for education topics is the British Education Index (BEI), which lists articles from journals about all aspects of education. Its coverage includes articles from pre-school to higher education, published in around 400 journal titles, and incorporates academic research and professional literature. While BEI is a subscription database, there is a free, open access version on the web, but it only lists the most recent references added to the database at www.bei.ac.uk.

Full-text databases – work in the same way as indexes and abstracting ones, but they also make the item accessible to you in pdf, Word or html format. Not all of the databases containing full-text material will provide it for every reference, and usually the numbers of journal titles that they cover is smaller than that of indexing and abstracting databases. Access is usually via the internet and password controlled. Be careful when searching full-text databases as your search is run against details of items on the database, as well as against the entire full-text content. If you search too generally this can mean your search terms are found in many places and you end up with lots of irrelevant results. So if possible search for your topic only in the title, abstract, and keyword or subject headings fields.

Science Direct (www.sciencedirect.com) is a good example of a full-text database. It is available to search as a guest via the internet and you can read abstracts of articles, but to be able to see the full text online your institution would need to have a subscription.

It is likely that you will need to search across a range of different databases to ensure you have done a comprehensive search of the literature available. Some databases will have better coverage than others and you will probably need advice from a subject librarian if you want to be thorough. Some starting points might be International Eric (incorporating BEI), Education Research Complete, ERIC (Education Resources Information Centre), Applied Social Science Index and Abstracts (ASSIA), International Bibliography of Social Sciences (IBSS), Web of Knowledge (incorporates Web of Science) and Zetoc.

Internet portals and gateways – these can often be a useful starting point for research on the web as they can help you to locate relevant materials more quickly than using a search engine. The organisers have already done the searching on the web, and have collected together the links to sites that they feel are of value to the researcher. Some good examples for education are:

Intute (www.intute.ac.uk) offers access to quality resources on the web for higher education that are organised and evaluated by subject specialists.

British Education Internet Resource Catalogue (www.beirc.ac.uk) offers access to information resources and services relevant to the study, practice and administration of education at a professional level.

The Teacher Training Resource Bank (www.ttrb.ac.uk) which is supported by the Training and Development Agency for Schools and provides access to research and evidence-based resources for teacher education. Again expert teacher educators from the UK have evaluated and compiled the material.

Many institutions have links on their library website pointing to gateways and portals that are of specific subject interest, so it is worth checking to see what is available.

Search engines – these are used to search the internet to find relevant material; the best known is Google (www.google.co.uk), but it is not the only one and although it is currently the largest search engine it does not cover the entire web. Some search engines allow you to search for a wide range of information types including images, blogs, maps and books. Metasearch engines (e.g. Dogpile – www.dogpile.com) allow you to search using more that one search engine at a time and retrieve aggregated results. They can be quite useful at widening out the results you retrieve and often help to organise the results in a variety of different ways.

Be aware that you will usually obtain a large number of results when you search the web, so you need to plan your searching, think carefully about how to search to find relevant material and ensure that you evaluate the results that you find.

Consult professionals

One of the biggest mistakes people make when they are searching for information is not choosing the right tools for the job. Until you are more confident about which information tools your institution offers, and what is appropriate for any given task, then take the advice of Hart who points out 'A good librarian can make all the difference to a search for relevant information' (Hart, 2001). Your subject specialist librarian will have up-to-date knowledge about the sources available in their library, the best ways to search them effectively, and a good working knowledge of their collections, so they can save you some valuable time. You can usually find contact details for your librarians on the library website.

If you are unclear about anything relating to your assignment then talk to your lecturers, and they can help to point you in the right direction. Make sure you have done some preparation before you go to see them or you will give the impression that you are expecting them to provide all the answers for you. Show them that you have started to engage with the material you have found and where you think you might need to look next.

If you are doing a dissertation you will probably be assigned a dissertation supervisor who you can use to give you guidance and advice. They will expect you to bring along materials that you have found as part of your searching and it will help if you can show them that you are organised and disciplined in your searching, so keep your records well organised in files that you can take with you if you have a tutorial.

Practical task

Identify the people who you can ask for help. Make a note of their names, contact details and times that they are available (tutors often have advertised office hours, librarians may run surgeries at certain times). If you need advice you will now know who to go to and how to find them when you need help.

Designing appropriate search strategies

Before you start to search for information it is important that you have a clear search strategy in place because you want to find relevant materials that add to the quality of your assignment. If you are systematic in your approach to searching, then you will be able to search a wide range of sources, manage your results easily, and make the most effective use of your time.

The first step is to make a list of the types of information you need to find, which will help you to decide which tools to use to find it. You can use this list to define the parameters of your search so you can set some boundaries to your research. Your assignment question or dissertation topic should offer you some guidance in this. Ask yourself about what you need.

- Is it a quick answer, or does it require more depth?

- Do you need up to date or historical information?

- Do you need primary or secondary information? Primary sources contain original material that research is based upon. Secondary sources have material that describes, analyses or discusses primary resources, and they represent the thinking of someone else.

- Do you only want English language material?

- What is your date range for publication of material? A good limit would be the last 5 or 10 years, unless your topic demands more.

- Do you only want research carried out in the UK or even just England?

- Do you want to find specific types of material e.g. statistics, news reports, etc?

If you are not familiar with the topic then look through textbooks and do some background reading, this will help you to discover the language that is used in relation to the topic. Ask yourself questions about the topic such as who, what, where, why, when and how. This will give some more areas that you might need to focus on, and it will also help you when you start to make up a list of search terms.

If you already have some knowledge of the topic is there anything that you need to check to validate it? It could be that the topic you are researching is new to you so you might want an overview of the material that is available in relation to your topic. This could be useful when you are trying to write your dissertation proposal and need to discover if there is enough information for your topic, or even too much. (Doing a *quick and dirty* search of the key resources for your subject area, using some relevant words as search terms should give you an overview of what is available. This will help you to plan more effectively as you will have an idea about how your search is likely to progress.)

It could be that you already know which material you need to access and *smart searching* in the appropriate resource can help to locate the item quickly and effectively. Use as much of the information that you already have available e.g. author, date, title, because this will mean it is easier for you to find the item that you want.

You might have a reading list for your course and this is a good starting point to help you find relevant materials. Use it intelligently though. Do not leave it to the last possible minute to do your research or you might find you cannot get access to the things you want quickly enough. For example, look for the items on your reading list. Some might already be out on loan and you need to reserve them. Others might have a booking system that allows you to choose a time when it is guaranteed you can have the item, or other items might be reference only and you need to find time to use them in the library. Resist the temptation to get everything on your reading list, especially if it is a long indicative list. You will just be swamped and find it difficult to work effectively.

You might have to carry out interviews or observations as part of your research and these need to be organised and the resulting paperwork or recordings have to be collated or transcribed, which will all take time to do. So it is a good idea to plan a schedule to fit everything in. Work backwards from the latest date you need the final material to work on and fit your timings around this.

What is different about searching for information about education?

Education is a field that is constantly evolving and new terminology regularly appears. For you as a researcher this can cause difficulties when you want to search for information, as you have to establish the latest terminology that is being used on the front line in education. You also need to know what has been used in the past to describe your topic. There are often inconsistencies in terminology between academic writers in education and this can present you with difficulties as well. Be aware that terminology may differ between countries so you need to know about the variations, but also words can have very different meanings. In the United States SATs is the Scholastic Assessment Test, which is used for college admissions, but in the United Kingdom the term has a different meaning and refers to the Standard Assessment Tests taken by primary and secondary school children.

Academics in education will often work with research level information, as well as theoretical material that looks back over the history of a topic, and covers education in more than just the country they are based in. Practitioners on the other hand produce materials that focus mainly on practice, and are applicable to their working environment, both in terms of the setting and the country they are in. They know their audience has more need of very current information about their area, such as the breaking news, changes in legislation or latest theories.

So it is essential that when you want to find information about an educational topic you research the language widely before you proceed to search any sources, and that you are aware that there will be different types of information targeted at different audiences.

Identifying key concepts and search terminology

If you are searching on electronic databases or search engines the results you retrieve will only be as good as the search terms you put in. These types of tools do not interpret information for you in any way. So to ensure your search is both comprehensive and effective you need to have a range of search terms to draw upon.

Start with your topic or assignment question and identify the key concepts (these are the significant words or ideas). For each concept you need to identify alternative terms (synonyms) that could be used to describe the concept, as these will form part of the list of words that you will use to search.

For example, take the concept of the teenager – some examples of synonymous terms for this could include adolescent, youth, juvenile, young person and adolescence.

You might find it helpful to compile a chart of the words or use a mind map (see Tony Buzan's books) if you prefer, as this will help you to be organised when you come to do your searching.

Remember that the terms you might use will not be the only ones in use, so be prepared for this. The topic you are researching might have been examined in a broader or narrower way than you are doing, but you still want to read that information, so make sure your search terms reflect this. There are a number of other issues that you need to consider and incorporate when you are compiling your key word list.

Generic words – some words have many different meanings and you might end up with lots of irrelevant information if you do not consider this, e.g. the word race.

Alternative spellings – many words have different spellings in their American and British form and you need to make sure that you search for all variations to maximise your results, e.g. behaviour/behavior.

Singular or plural terms – some words just need an *s* added to the end to become a plural, but in other cases the plural and singular words differ quite a lot, so have both terms in your list e.g. woman/women.

Abbreviations or acronyms – practitioners or specialists in their field often use abbreviations, but make sure you search for the full term as well; you can never be sure which has been used e.g. SEN/special educational needs.

Alternative word endings – make sure you do not miss words that stem from the word that you are looking for. For example if you are looking for the word *child* then childish, children and children's would be relevant as well.

Avoid words that are too general such as education, management, technology. Try to think of more specific terms in relation to these words e.g. primary education, classroom behaviour management.

Remember that there are no right or wrong keywords. They act as a framework to help you search for the information that you need to find. Be prepared to be flexible with your search terms as there will be variation in what you have to use in different tools. It is also important that when you find materials that match your requirements, you are always open to the possibility of finding additional search terms in the text that you had not thought of, or even come across before. This is known as *harvesting*, and will allow you to search further and narrow the field of potentially missed material.

Worked example

Identifying your initial search terms

The task

You have been given the following essay title:

> *Discuss whether gender affects success in maths, in primary schools.*

Look at how you would identify a list of the key concepts; try to think of some keywords for searching as well as alternatives such as synonyms, singular and plural words, abbreviations, etc.

The main concepts to identify from the essay title are: *gender, success, maths* and *primary schools*. If you take each one individually and unpick it a little you can start to build some search term possibilities.

1. Gender

As well as using this search term, each gender can be searched for individually e.g. boy or girl, male or female or there might be a broader discussion about gender differences or sex differences. You might also find articles referring to gender bias in teaching or education that could provide useful information.

2. Success

This term offers a range of opportunities for searching. You might want to try alternative words such as achievement, performance or attainment. SATs results or tests and testing might be further options. Broader terminology could include school tests, national tests or even exams. You would also have to consider the possibility that writers might have explored the topic from a much more negative viewpoint and so terms like underachievement or failure might be useful to list.

3. Maths

This is one of those words that offers up many alternatives such as mathematics, mathematics teaching, mathematics education or mathematical (we will explore how we can search for words with the same stem in a more effective way in the next chapter). In addition, schools talk about the numeracy strategy or numeracy framework.

4. Primary schools

This is a plural, so consider the singular term. This is another term that has many other options when it comes to searching, such as infants and juniors, Key Stages 1 (or one) and 2 (or two) (this is often abbreviated to KS1 and KS2) and more general discussions might just talk about primary education.

As information changes constantly and is updated so are the search terms that you may need to use to find it. The suggestions above are only a guide; it would be impossible to provide a prescriptive list of terms. Remember that the sources you use will influence the search terms you choose as well, so newspapers for example are more likely to use words that the general public are familiar with e.g. primary school rather than Key Stages, or tests rather than attainment levels.

We have already discussed the importance of thinking and planning before the actual searching even begins, and the above task indicates how much time may be needed just to unpick a fairly short assignment title. Having a variety of search terminology to use will ensure that you do not miss key material when you do start searching. It will also give you alternatives to use in the event of no results being returned when you search on a database. This is often the time when students panic if they do not have a backup plan, especially if they are already feeling out of their depth using an unfamiliar resource such as a subject database. You might be lucky and find what you need to straightaway, but it definitely helps to be prepared.

How do you obtain the information you need?

Some fairly simple preparation can help to make the process of searching for information easier and prevent any nasty surprises or delays for you later on. So spending some time finding out about what sources of information your institution provides access to, checking out how you obtain access and if you need any separate passwords or login details, means you are prepared. Establish how the access to computers is organised if you do not have your own. Are there any you can book at specific times or can you borrow a laptop? Make sure you know about the printing and photocopying procedures so you can start to collect material as you find it, which you can read later on.

What happens if you find some good references when you are searching for information for your assignment or presentation, but you find that your library does not hold them? First consider if you are looking for more information than you really need to. Tutors usually ensure that there are adequate resources available to complete assignments set as part of taught courses. Are you struggling to find what you need because you have left your research too late? If most of the materials have already been borrowed from the library, then talk to your subject librarian about finding alternatives. They might be able to point you to electronic books or other full-text sources that are still available.

If you are doing a dissertation however, your library may not cover the subject you are investigating in as much breadth as you need, so what options are open to you when you know an item exists, which you want to read, but your library does not have it?

Inter-library loans or document supply

There is a national scheme in the United Kingdom that allows you obtain materials from other libraries that are not held at your home library. You will usually have to fill in a request form from your library (this might be printed or electronic), and sign a copyright declaration, and then your library will make the request on your behalf. You do not need to try to work out who has the materials as most requests go to the British Library Document Supply Centre in the first instance.

Visiting other institutions and collections

There might be a number of reasons why inter-library loans are not appropriate when you are trying to access materials not in your library. Time might be a factor. You need the material quickly and you know it is in a nearby university library or collection. You may just want to browse across a wider range of material in a library that specialises in your subject area or discipline.

How do you find out about other collections and which libraries hold what? Both the HERO (www.hero.ac.uk) and *UK Active Map of Universities and HE Institutions* (www.scit.wlv.ac.uk/ukinfo/) websites include access points to all HE sector libraries. They are useful sites if you are planning a trip to another institution as you can search through their library catalogue to see if they have what you want before you travel there, saving you wasted time. It is always worth checking that the library is open on the day you want to visit, that you are not restricted to vacation only times as a visitor, and make a note of the opening times, etc. Do not just assume you can visit and access anywhere. Most HE libraries' websites will include information for visitors. Another useful site to offer guidance about access is the Sconul website (www.sconul.ac.uk). Look at the 'using other libraries' section to find out more about visiting other libraries.

To find out about specialist libraries, archives or collections there are a number of places you could look; if your library purchases *The ASLIB directory of information sources* in the United Kingdom use the extensive subject index to locate possible collections. You can also do a Google search, as many specialist collections have a website presence (remember to narrow your search to UK locations though).

Selecting material

When you start compiling the material and information that you want to use in your assignments remember to look at it and judge how useful it is to you, as well at its relevance to the topic you are researching.

Relevance

Is the material relevant to your topic? It is easy to be distracted by material that looks interesting, but it sits on the edge of your topic, and is not relevant.

What will you use the information for? Is it background material or does it give you specific information of precise detail, or can you use it as a lead to find other relevant materials?

Use the date as an indicator, but not total decider, of relevance. Older does not necessarily mean that something is no longer of use.

How will you use the information? Does it provide you with evidence or examples that you can use to support existing ideas?

Read the abstract if there is one, read a review of a book if you can or a synopsis (use Google as a search tool to get access to these).

Authority

If you find research that is cited time and again throughout your range of references then it is likely to be seen as quality by other researchers, and therefore worth consulting. Even if the material is not the most up to date available, it is the eminence of the author that gives it relevance. A good example in educational terms is Piaget. Look at the source of the material and the author's standing in the field of knowledge, as well as the intended audience.

Be harsh

Ask yourself whether this material is essential or if it just restates what you have found out from other material. If it is evidential, is it the best or strongest piece that you have read? Is the level consistent with the rest of the information you are using (or is it too complex or even too simplistic)? If it does not add anything to your work then do not use it. It is very easy to be carried away with the process and sense of achievement when searching for and finding information. Just because you found a piece of information does not mean you have to use it.

Keeping up to date

The pace of change in information technology is very rapid. Make it a priority to keep the skills that you are learning up to date, as most of them will be transferable to other aspects of your home and working life. You can also use these skills to find out about emerging technologies, and make decisions about how applicable they could be for you. Ensure that you know what your institution can offer in the way of search tools and resources and if anything new is added make it a priority to find out if it is of use to you.

You can keep yourself up to date with news about education by accessing a quality daily newspaper; some have sections devoted specifically to education (e.g. *The Guardian* on Tuesdays). You might want to browse regularly or subscribe to a particular magazine or journal that covers your area of study e.g. *The Times Educational Supplement (TES)*. Remember that this does not necessarily mean you will be using a paper source; many newspapers and journals have websites with electronic content. A great example is the TES website (www.tes.co.uk) where you can read parts of the original paper for free as well as searching the extensive archive of articles.

If you are doing a dissertation you will be working over several months and will want to check for any relevant new information that is published over that time. There are a number of useful tools available to save you having to repeat your searches.

Alerting or current awareness services help researchers keep up to date by sending them automatic email alerts when new information about a particular subject or topic is made available. These alerting services are available for many different types of material and sources, including journals, and subscription databases. To receive email alerts to the table of contents from the journal and conference holdings of the British Library try the Zetoc alerting service (http://zetoc.mimas. ac.uk/), if your institution subscribes.

You can save your searches in many databases and run them again at a later date, but in other databases your search will be run automatically on a regular basis and the results emailed to you.

The Web of Science database (http://wok.mimas.ac.uk/) allows you to create citation alerts. If you have found an article of interest you can be alerted by email or an RSS feed when someone else cites the article in another published source.

You can be alerted when there are changes or updates made to websites. The Intute website (www.intute.ac.uk) sends a weekly email that lists any new websites it has added to its database that match what you want. Google also offers alerts like this, but think very carefully about how much material you could receive, even if your search is well designed.

News feeds or RSS feeds are a different way of receiving information. For example rather than checking the BBC website for news, you can subscribe to their RSS feed, and every time a new article is added to the website it will be added to a newsreader that you have installed on your computer. You can set up these feeds from a number of different websites and they will all feed into your newsreader. Many electronic journals now provide news feeds for their contents pages.

Blogs are rapidly increasing in number and can be produced by both individuals and institutions. They can be a good way of gaining insight into what experts or specialists are talking about in relation to current topics in a certain field of knowledge. But remember nobody reviews blog entries, so you will need to do some evaluation of your own to decide the quality of material you are viewing. Technorati (http://technorati.com/) is a useful search engine for finding blogs.

You could also join a mailing list where researchers in your subject area discuss ideas, share information and advertise events and conferences. JISCmail (www.jiscmail.ac.uk) hosts a large number of academic related lists. You can join a list and receive all the postings made to it directly to your email, or you can just search through the archives for relevant postings.

Summary of key points

Use the subject specialist librarians to give you guidance. You will not be making a nuisance of yourself. Their job is to help staff and students gain access to the resources they need.

Remember that there are no right or wrong keywords when you are trying to make up your list. The list will develop as you search and you will find more terms to add to it as you go, and some of the words on the list initially will probably not be used.

It is a good idea to keep the search plans that you draw up, as some of the terminology that you use for one piece of work might be needed again, and it will save you having to try to remember what worked well last time for a particular topic.

There are often additions to the range of research tools available to you through your institution's library. So keep up to date with what is available by looking out for emails, flyers or sessions that are offered by the library.

References and further reading

Hart, C. (2001) *Doing a literature search*. London: Sage.

Buzan, T. (1993) *The mind map book*. London: BBC Books.

Reynard, K.W. and Reynard, M.E. (eds) (2008) *The Aslib directory of information sources in the United Kingdom*. 15th ed. London: Aslib.

4. Locating and accessing information

Practical advice on how to search for and identify information from a wide variety of sources.

Learning outcomes

Having worked through this chapter you should be better able to:

- understand the wide variety of information sources available and be able to locate and select the best ones for any given task;

- know how to locate the sources you need by using the appropriate tools;

- search effectively and efficiently across a wide range of tools;

- evaluate the results of searches to establish their relevance.

Sources of information, which to use and how to find them

In the previous chapter we looked at how the types of information you need to find will be governed by what sort of assignment you are doing, and its topic area. You now need to familiarise yourself with the sources that are available to you through your library and this will help you to decide which tools you should use to find your information. We will have a look at different types of sources, discuss when they would be relevant for you to use and outline strengths and weakness of them as an information source.

There are a wide range of sources that offer you access to information and these range from very general information aimed at the widest audience possible, through to very specific information that is targeted at specialists in the field. When you are conducting a search for information for assignments or dissertations, it is usual to start with general background information and then move on to find more specific and recent sources.

Reflective task

Identifying sources you have used

Try listing any different types of resources that you may have used to find information. Consider any issues you had with using them such as access, understanding and the type of information that they gave you.

Have a look through the different resources listed below and see if there are other resources you were unaware of, or if there are issues that you had not considered before in relation to the particular types of resources. Compare your list with the one below.

Books will give you good background information for your topic. They are often wide ranging in their content, are particularly good for qualitative information in education and usually they contain bibliographies (reference lists) which offer a starting point for you to work from. However, books can take a long time to be published so the currency of the information that they provide can be a problem. Nowadays books can be in both paper and electronic formats and the starting point when searching for them is your Library catalogue. Book titles are often misleading, so be sure to look at the contents pages to get a clear idea of coverage.

Remember – library catalogues only have details about the book's title, not the content. General books on your topic might have chapters that focus on areas more deeply than the title suggests. E-books might be listed in other collections and not on the library catalogue, so make sure you are aware of what your library offers.

If you are doing a dissertation, you will want to find out about all relevant books that have been published, and whether your library has them or not. Search the British Library catalogue (http://catalogue.bl.uk) – the British Library is a national deposit library and has copies of all works published in the UK, or try COPAC (http://copac.ac.uk). This is a union catalogue which searches the catalogues of some of the biggest research libraries in the UK, including the Institute of Education. The online bookseller Amazon is a useful place to search (make sure you are searching the book section though), as you can view scanned copies of the contents and index pages of some of the books it lists and these can help you to decide whether to pursue access to the item or not.

Access to books can sometimes be problematic; with paper based titles your library needs to hold the ones you want to read, otherwise you will need to try to access it elsewhere (see Chapter 3 for document delivery). E-books require your library to have a subscription and that means you will need a password to access them. Use the contents page and index to help you search efficiently and effectively. Remember to think about terminology. You might need to be more or less specific about the terms you search for (as we discussed in the previous chapter). Consider who the author and publisher of books are, as a way of establishing authority. Check that the book is still current (i.e. the latest edition), and establish if there have there been any major developments in the field you are researching that have happened since the book was written.

Journals – are publications that appear in a series and are published at regular intervals (this could be weekly, monthly or annually), and they contain a collection of articles. Journals are sometimes known as serials, periodicals or magazines and, like books, can be paper or electronic in format.

Journals are most useful because they provide up-to-date information about the latest developments in fields of research or professional practice because they are published regularly. They allow very focused research to be published as they have a very targeted audience. Often there is an abstract provided, which you can read first to work out if the article covers the area you are interested in. There are different types of journals:

Scholarly or academic journals – academic journals assume specialist knowledge and use specific terminology or vocabulary; usually there are no pictures, unless they are illustrating an aspect of the text. Academic journal articles will usually have extensive bibliographies (reference lists), which can be a great help to the researcher. The authors that are chosen for publication add to the credibility of the journal and will often publish frequently in the same titles. The strength of journal articles is that the short length allows the ability to focus on one or two specific aspects of a topic. However, this is also their weakness in comparison with books that offer a broader overview. Some scholarly journals are peer-reviewed – this means the articles are scrutinised before publication by other experts in the field of knowledge. This gives the journal and the material in it greater academic credibility. Whilst journals are published regularly, and are therefore more current than books, there is still likely to be a delay in publishing if the title is one where the articles undergo peer review.

Professional/trade/practitioner journals – this type of journal offers the opportunity for theory to be put into practice and be reported on for others in the same profession to learn from. They provide valuable updates on current issues in the profession, and whilst they are generally not publishing original research they often look at how to apply other people's published research. Articles are usually shorter in length than in academic journals, are written by professionals in the field and the level of language is geared to the professional who has a degree of expertise in the areas covered, so you will often find that acronyms or specialised language are used. There are often few, if any, references because the articles are looking at practical application. Professional journals are often illustrated with photos and include job adverts and useful products for sale to a target audience.

Popular (e.g. magazines) – the level of material in these titles is geared to a general audience of interested people but they offer little in the way of original research. Material is rarely written by people with authority. There are usually no references beyond a few websites and they are often heavy with pictures. (They are financed by advertising revenue.)

Practical task

Find a scholarly journal and a practitioner journal that your university subscribes to and look for the characteristics described above. Compare the articles in the journals and think about the types of information they offer and how both have their place in the right context.

Most academic libraries do not allow paper journals to be borrowed so you will usually need to photocopy any articles you want, or check if there is an electronic version available that you can use online or print from.

If you are doing a dissertation, you will often need articles from a wide range of journals and there is no guarantee that your library will have access to all the titles that you need articles from, so you might need to order them using inter-library loans, or make a visit to a library that has the title.

If you have a reference for a journal article, check to see if your library holds the title of the journal, and how you access it (i.e. is it in paper or electronic).

To find out where other articles on your topic have been published you will need to use an index or abstracting tool (discussed in Chapter 3); these will usually be electronic (databases). Do not forget that some databases link to the full text of the article references that you find, but others will just have bibliographic details, or an abstract.

Conference papers – can be an excellent source for information about the latest research in a subject area. Researchers often use conferences as a opportunity to present their research findings to their peers. They can provide very up to date information about research if they are at the pre-publication stage. They are also a good way of finding out who the experts in your subject area are (then you can check to see what else they have published before); and conferences are usually themed, so if you have a reference to a conference paper and there are published proceedings then there might be other useful papers in the collection. The best places to find conference papers are databases such as Zetoc (http://zetoc.mimas.ac.uk/) (higher education access only) and Education-line (www.leeds.ac.uk/educol/), or you might find details about conference material on the website of research organisations and associations.

Newspapers – are useful because they record events and public opinion. They cover recent developments before articles are published in journals, but you need to be careful about the lack of objectivity and bias found in newspaper reporting. Be wary of the educational supplements in the broadsheet titles, as journalists, rather than educationalists often write the content. The editorials can give you insight into current debates in education, but they do not have the authority of the latest research published in journals. Your library may subscribe to online databases such as LexisNexis Butterworths or Newsbank, which both have holdings for a large number of news titles in full-text, but you will need a password to access them.

Theses and dissertations – if you are writing a dissertation, or thesis, it is useful to be able to see some examples of previous submissions to look at layout, see how others have approached research, or to look at a subject relevant bibliography. Many university libraries will keep some sample copies for you to browse through. To search for dissertations and theses written at other institutions, try using the British Library Catalogue (narrow your search using the words *thesis* or *theses* or *dissertation*), or try *Index to Theses* if your institution has a subscription. This is a database containing details of PhDs and some masters theses submitted at UK Universities since 1716.

Audio-visual sources – are a valuable primary source that should not be forgotten. One of the most useful innovations for all those involved in teaching and schools is Teachers' TV, a concept that was developed by the Department for Education and Skills as a way for teachers and schools to learn from each other. It broadcasts on a free to air channel and many of the programmes are available to watch again from the website (www.teachers.tv).

Oral sources – can provide very valuable insights into an area that you had previously not explored through other sources. In the field of education there are three main categories of people that could provide you with this information:

1. Professionals – these could be lecturers who are experts in their chosen field, or a conference speaker presenting a paper. These can include government-based agencies such as the DCFS or TDA, or in the school setting, head teachers, teaching assistants or teacher mentors.

2. Parents – a hugely valuable source who have a very vested interest in what is happening in education from the top down, as it affects their children directly.

3. Pupils – potentially the most valuable resource of all. They are able to provide experiences and evidence from education as it is now. They are the most acutely affected people of all when it comes to changes in teaching practice, government policy, etc.

The type of information you can gain from these sources will vary hugely and will be dependent on the methods you use to retrieve it, and whether it is subjective or objective.

The internet as a source – remember to differentiate between the things that you find on the web itself and those things that you find through subscription databases that are hosted on the web. The material in the databases has usually been collected and reviewed and had added value given to it often by academics or experts in the field of knowledge. With the web there is often no organiser or evaluator and you have to be extra careful about ensuring you evaluate the material that you find. We have mentioned gateways and portals that exist to help, but there will be times when these do not provide you with what you were hoping to find and you need to search intelligently using search engines to find what you want.

There is an amazing amount of potentially useful information on the web, freely available and in full text. Government departments routinely load the full text of reports, documentation and statistics on to their websites and the sites are usually well organised. However, when you are searching for government-based information on the web it helps to have some knowledge about how education is organised and who is responsible for which aspects, otherwise you can waste a lot of time chasing round in circles.

Worked example

The task

You are asked to prepare for a debate in a week's time, based around this statement:

> *There is a belief that children, in schools today, have a limited educational diet focused on getting them through the SATs tests, and teachers are both under-used and demoralised.*

You will be arguing in agreement with this statement, and are allowed to make a five-minute presentation at the start of the debate, as is the opposition. The main debate that follows will last for 20 minutes.

Which sources of information would you use to find information to support this exercise?

Start by working out what you already know and where your knowledge gaps are. For example, are you clear about the SATs, what they are and what ages children sit them? You probably need information about the history of testing and current practice, easy to follow arguments, clear data to back up your arguments, academic research, studies, experiences from the front-line – teachers, parents, students. Do not forget to consider the argument from the other side, as this will help you as well.

1. Books

These will be good for the history and background to the National Curriculum and testing, and as the current position has existed for a while there will be texts that look at the issues raised.

2. Journals

Academic titles may have details of research that has been carried out. There might be statistical data about success rates (do not spend too much time on these though as you are limited in your research time and it could take a while to look at academic articles). Practitioner or professional journals may have articles that give insight from the teachers' point of view, or discuss strategies they have to employ to teach for the SATs.

3. Newspapers

Debates about the annual SATs test are always in the newspapers in May (test time) and August (results time) each year, and there could be references to studies or reports in these articles. Check the education section of the broadsheets, as well as specific titles like the *TES*.

4. Websites

Try government websites for information and links to the bodies involved with testing. But also remember to try out gateways such as Intute, to save wasting too much time searching.

5. Oral sources

These could provide powerful examples of the voices of professionals, parents and children. You might find blogs or opinions posted on sites that are looking at educational issues like this one. Remember to establish the quality of the website though.

How to search (including Boolean)

Learning how to search effectively and efficiently can be a slow process but remember you are learning valuable transferable skills that will be useful to you in other arenas. We have already discussed search strategies in the previous chapter as well as how to break your topic down into concepts and keywords, and compile a range of search terms to use. But how do you actually search using these terms, in the most effective way, to find the information that you need? Electronic resources are all quite similar in the way that they allow you to search, whether you are using an internet search engine like Google or a subject specific database like the British Education Index. They will let you combine search terms together and refine the results you achieve, although the way in which each source offers this may vary.

When you search a tool for a topic just try your main search term first and then adjust your search in response to the results you achieve. There is no point wasting valuable time constructing complicated searches when the tool you are using may only have a few items of value to you, and you would have found them quite quickly initially by just using one or two of your main search terms.

Boolean logic

It is very common when you search for information that you get too many results, or results that are not relevant. If you know how to combine your search terms together effectively you can achieve better results.

Boolean logic uses the operators AND, OR and NOT to combine your search terms together and make your search more effective. If we look at each one individually we can see how it can be used to help you.

AND – If your initial search has retrieved lots of results narrow them down by using the Boolean AND (e.g. boys AND maths). What the AND is doing is looking for references where both of your search terms appear, so your results will be more targeted and relevant. In this case all your results will be about boys and maths, not just one or other of the topics on their own.

OR – If you have retrieved very few or no results then first check your spelling. Next try alternative terms from your list and widen your search out. Use the Boolean OR operator to help (e.g. university OR college). This will look for references that contain either one, or both of your terms, so your results are broader. OR helps you find references with synonyms or related terms in them.

NOT – If you have too many results after you have tried to use AND and OR look at your results to see if there are keywords or concepts that you could eliminate using the Boolean NOT (e.g. science NOT girls). This is a more difficult operator to use as you can end up excluding some results that could prove useful if you are not too careful.

For a good visual example of how Boolean logic works see the Boolean Machine website: http://kathyschrock.net/rbs3k/boolean/

Brackets – If you are searching with quite a complex combination of keywords, or you are using more that one Boolean operator in your searching then brackets () can often be used to add clarity. The brackets make sure that the right search terms are grouped together; you might find your search does not work in the way you expected if you did not do this, as different databases might prioritise the order of searches for the Boolean operators, for example, science and (assessment or testing) not (higher or secondary).

Truncation symbols – are available in many online databases. They allow you to search for the stem of a word and find all the variable endings that it might have. The most common truncation symbol is the asterix (*), but it is not universal, so check your source.

For example, searching for educat* will give you results that include educate, educating, education, educational, educator, educators, etc.

Be careful though not to shorten your word too far or you might get many extra irrelevant terms (e.g. if you were searching for words to do with computers and computing do not truncate to just comp* or you will find terms like competition and companion are included in your results).

Wildcards – are an option in some databases. Use them to replace any single letter (e.g. wom?n finds woman or women). You can use these symbols at the beginning of a word or in the middle to look for alternative spellings.

Phrase searching – is supported in some databases and search engines. Sometimes the default is a phrase search if you enter two search terms side by side, or there may be a tick box option; in other databases you can use inverted commas around the phrase to force the words to be searched for in the order you want and together. Beware though as some databases will automatically insert an AND or an OR between two terms if you do not include anything.

You do not always want to search for just a phrase, but you want the terms used to be near each other in the source, or even in the same paragraph or sentence. Some databases offer proximity searching. There are variations between search tools and you will need to look at the database help to see what it offers.

Field searching – in databases is often available. This is when you tell the database where you want your words to appear (e.g. in the article title, or keywords). Be careful to use this option if it is available when you are using full-text databases as most words will appear somewhere in the text of an article for example, but they may have little or no relevance to your search, so be clear about where you want you search terms to appear.

Many databases have some form of *controlled vocabulary*. This can help you when you have many alternatives for your topic and are not sure which one will be used with which tool. Different databases have different approaches to this. Some have subject headings, or descriptors, whilst others offer a thesaurus or browsable index. Check the help pages on the database to see what it offers and use the feature to help you search more effectively and retrieve the results you want that are focused on the topic you want.

Beware

Sometimes letter case is important in some tools, so your Boolean operators may need to be in capitals to avoid being ignored. You really need to make sure that you understand how your search tool works to get the best from it, but you also need to be aware that not all search tools are the same or offer the same functionality, or if they do it might not be offered in the same way in each tool.

Limiting your search further – it can be useful sometimes to limit your search results further without affecting the search terms (keywords) that you have used. The trick is to limit only as you need to. Databases will usually have a number of ways to allow you to limit results further, such as:

- language, which allows you to retrieve items only in languages you can read;

- date of publication helps you to avoid older materials – be sure that date limiting applies to publication date, and not the date that the record of the item was added to the tool you are searching;

- particular types of documents such as book chapters, journals articles or conference papers if relevant;

- full text only: can be useful if that is an option and you need material you can use straight away – remember to look through the non full-text results later to be more thorough;

- by named publication i.e. limiting your search results to things from just one publication, e.g. only articles about your topic that are published in the *British Journal of Educational Psychology*; it is useful when you know your library holds a journal title and you can access it easily;

- web search engines such as Google also have some very useful limiting facilities in their advanced search options like types of format and domain restrictions (i.e. the type of website the material comes from – for example websites with the domain *.ac.uk* belong to higher education academic institutions in the United Kingdom).

Databases often offer the choice to sort your results, including sorting by date, author or source (everything is grouped according to the publication they originate from), which can be a useful way to start if you have a number of results to review.

This is quite an exhaustive list and is used to demonstrate that there are many options available for you to enable intelligent searching, and to save you time wading through unhelpful results.

Evaluation of results

Whenever you do a search using an online resource such as a database or internet search engine it is important that you assess the effectiveness of your search results, in order to decide how you are going to progress next. Decide if the results of the search are what you expected and if they meet your needs. Is there information missing that you expected to retrieve, or is there information that you were not expecting to find and now want to exclude? You may wish to modify your search based on the outcome of this process.

What problems have you encountered with your results, and what action can you take? If you have too many results you could:

- narrow your search – add more keywords;

- be more specific e.g. try key stage one, instead of primary education;

- use phrase searches e.g. 'curriculum planning';

- add limits – document type, date, full text only.

If you have too few results you could:

- widen your search using synonyms;

- make your search terms less specific;

- use truncation or wildcards in case of spelling problems;

- split up phrase searches to look for the words near each other instead.

If your results seem irrelevant try:

- excluding irrelevant search terms using NOT searches;

- adding limits such as date or document type to narrow results.

If you did not retrieve any results try:

- checking for spelling errors;

- asking for help in choosing the correct database;

- ensuring your limits are not too restrictive, removing them one at a time;

- browsing indexes/thesauruses to see if there are more appropriate terms;

- changing your search terms to more general ones.

Ask yourself if you are you being realistic. Is the information too current to be published anywhere other than newspapers? Does the information you are trying to find exist only in one place? You might need to search in a variety of sources and extract relevant material from a number of sources to compile a wider view of the topic.

This evaluation exercise is just in relation to the results of your searching and not the quality or appropriateness of the material they point to. That is a process that you will have to complete once you have the results you need, and is covered in depth in Chapter 5.

It is quite likely that you will need to amend and refine your search strategy and run your searches a number of times before you retrieve items that match your requirements. This does not mean you are bad at searching, it shows an awareness that searching is a complex process and is something that requires perseverance and effort to be effective.

Record keeping with a purpose

Get into the habit of good record keeping throughout the research process. Keep a record of which search terms/words you used. They might be useful in future searches. Note which Boolean terms worked well and list the search tools that you used. You could print out the search results page as this will help you get used to the types of information and subject coverage of databases. It is also useful to note the date when you did the searching, because new material is being added to databases on a daily basis, so if you are researching for your dissertation it is likely that you will rerun your search on a number of occasions to ensure you capture anything new that has been added.

Ensure you have bibliographic details for everything you use; you will need them to compile your reference list at the end of the assignment. Your institution might use referencing software like Endnote or Refworks. If you have your own computer you may be able to have a student version loaded on to it for you to manage your references. For web based materials you might find it easier to bookmark sites, or use web based bookmarking sites like del.icio.us – http://del.icio.us/. You can log in to this wherever you are using the internet to access your personal bookmarks. Keep track of reservations or inter-library loan requests you have made in case you have questions to ask in the library.

It might seem laborious and time consuming to be doing all of this planning preparation and organising, but it will help you in the long run. The more proficient you become, the less time you will waste in the future, trying to track down what you need. An added bonus is that the skills you are using are ones that can be used when you are searching for things that are not just for your studies, i.e. transferable skills.

Finally

The areas that we have covered in the last two chapters are very practical ones. If you consider these six steps each time you start a search for information, whether it is for an assignment or in response to any other information need then you should be successful in your outcomes.

1. Analyse your problem or question and define what you need to find.

2. Identify your information sources and the tools needed to search.

3. Construct your search terminology.

4. Search using effective search statements.

5. Evaluate what you find and decide if you need to search further.

6. Refine and repeat your searching until you have found what you need.

Summary of key points

Know your sources and what type of information they provide, as this will guide you to which search tools to use.

It is a good idea to practise planning and executing searches as often as you can, even when you are looking for information for a personal need, not related to your study. Practice really does help you to improve your skills.

It is very important to use the help available on a database or search engine to avoid problems and save you time if you are not clear about its search protocols.

Keep records all the time so you know what you have already done.

Allow yourself plenty of time. Planning and searching for information is not a quick process.

References and further reading

If you need further advice, or help to improve your searching skills, then start with your own institution. See if there are sessions, handouts or information on its website. If you search on the web you will be able to find a broad selection of sites from other academic institutions offering examples of searches and advice.

5. Evaluating information

Information literate students critically evaluate the information that they find and the methods that they use to find it.

Learning outcomes

Having worked through this chapter you should be better able to:

- **assess the usefulness and significance of the information that you find by selecting and applying appropriate evaluation criteria;**

- **use information from different sources in order to achieve a synthesis (i.e. your own understanding) of the main ideas that you have identified;**

- **determine whether or not your information needs have been met, or if further searching is required.**

The importance of being critical

Information searching is often an ongoing process rather than a single step on the way to task completion. For example, when you are drafting the conclusion to an essay you may find that you need some additional information in order to emphasise an important point. Similarly, in the case of a dissertation you may start writing the *review of literature* before you have identified all of the literature that you will include in your review. However, irrespective of the stage at which you identify a potential information source, you should still take the time to evaluate it before you decide whether or not to use it.

This applies as much to oral sources as it does to books, journals and the internet. In other words, all of your course-related information gathering should be guided by critical reading (or listening) as well as by critical thinking, rather than unquestioning acceptance of what you are told.

This does not mean that you should question everything that you read or hear, but to effectively evaluate information you must bear in mind that some of what you find will not be objective truth. Even good writers and speakers have biases and they often mix fact with opinion. If you are to identify bias and distinguish between fact and opinion you must be critical, that is, you must make judgements about the reliability of your information sources.

In the case of printed text you may find that you agree with what the author has written because it is consistent with your existing knowledge of the subject; disagree because it is inconsistent with your existing knowledge; or conclude that you need further information before you can make an informed judgement. When you read in this way you are reading critically and if you adopt the same approach during lectures, for example, you will be listening critically, i.e. utilising the same skills. As you develop these skills you will also become better at critical thinking.

Unless you are thinking critically you will be unable to effectively evaluate the information that you find. Some guidance on how to do this is included in the next section and, while practice may not make you perfect, it should make you better. However, before considering how to evaluate information sources I suggest that you spend a few minutes reflecting upon what is meant by critical thinking.

Reflective task

What is critical thinking?

The Qualifications and Curriculum Authority describes critical thinking as a crucial aspect of learning 'that should permeate the curriculum and the life of the school' (QCA, 2008). This implies that if you intend to work in schools you should have a clear understanding of what it means to think critically.

It may further your understanding if you compare what you think it means with the definition in the glossary of the *Thinking skills* section of *The Standards site*. Since this definition is endorsed by the Department for Children, Schools and Families, you may regard it as authoritative.

Critical thinking is:

> *the process of determining the authenticity, accuracy, or value of something; characterised by the ability to seek reasons and alternatives, perceive the complete situation, and change one's view based on evidence and reasoning. Sometimes also called analytical or convergent thinking. Often related to formal or informal logic and to reasoning.*
>
> (DCSF, 2008)

Hopefully your definition will not be not too dissimilar, but if it is you may wish to reconsider it. My purpose was not to get you to test your understanding but to draw your attention to the direct connection between critical thinking and the *process of determining the authenticity, accuracy and value of information*.

Assessing the usefulness and significance of information

In order to ensure that you are logical and methodical when you assess information sources you must be able to select and apply appropriate evaluation criteria to them. It was suggested in Chapter 2 that your tutors will normally expect you to use information that is accurate, up to date, unbiased and the work of acknowledged experts; but sometimes you may have to consider other criteria and these may vary in relation to the tasks in which you are engaged and the sources that you have identified. Thus, there can be no definitive checklist of evaluation criteria and you are advised to be flexible in your approach, selecting those that you think are the most appropriate for your particular purpose.

Rumsey (2004) suggests that you assess websites in terms of their ownership, authority, currency, quality of content, and intended audience; while for published sources she recommends that you use provenance, content, relation to the subject, and access and use.

In addition, many university libraries produce their own guidelines on evaluating information, some of which are available online. The library website at Cornell University, for example, offers some very user-friendly guidance. This can be accessed via any of the major search engines by typing in *Cornell evaluating sources help pages*'. You may also wish to find out what your institution's library advises, since the better informed you are about evaluation criteria the better you will be at assessing the usefulness and significance of your information sources.

Practical task

Selecting criteria for evaluating information

Access and read the *Evaluating web resources* help page at Cornell University Library and note the six guidelines (criteria) that it recommends for evaluating websites, i.e. currency, authority, reliability, purpose, coverage, style and functionality. This should only take a few minutes. (If you need the URL it can be found in the appropriate entry in the references and further reading list at the end of the chapter.)

Compare these criteria with the five that Rumsey (2004, p. 168) advocates for the evaluation of websites, i.e. ownership, authority, currency, quality of content, and intended audience. As you can see, there are some similarities as well as differences between the two sets of criteria. If your institution's library recommends its own criteria you may wish to include them in your comparison.

Now decide which of these criteria you think would be the most helpful if you were evaluating a website. The decision is important since you cannot assess information sources logically and methodically unless you have a method. Your decision should not preclude your being flexible in your choice.

Once you have decided upon your main criteria, 'evaluation can take the form of a series of pertinent questions' (Rumsey 2004, p. 188) which relate to these criteria. While your questioning must be systematic and objective, it should not take up too much time, i.e. you should do it efficiently. Therefore it is the pertinence of the questions that you use to evaluate information sources that matters, rather than the number.

Although your choice of questions will vary in relation to your changing information needs and the different types of source that you evaluate, you may find some of the following examples helpful when you try to formulate your own questions. The criteria to which these questions relate are indicated alongside them and, like the questions themselves, they are intended as a prompt to help you to work out your own approach.

Printed sources

In the case of a book you may decide to ask:

Provenance

- Is it from a reputable academic publisher?

- Is the author a recognised authority on the subject?

- Is it a major work in the subject area?

Access

- Can I obtain a copy quickly and easily?

Currency

- Is it the most recent edition?

Content

- Do the table of contents and index suggest that it contains sufficient relevant information for my needs?

- Does it have an impressive bibliography or reference list (e.g. Is it well-researched?) and, if not, should I trust it?

- How do the author's main ideas compare with those of others who have written about the subject? (e.g. Does the book appear to be biased or does it present an interesting alternative interpretation?).

Intended audience

- What is its intended audience? (e.g. Is it too specialist or too general for my purposes?)

In the case of a journal article you may decide to ask:

Provenance

- Has it been published in a reputable academic journal?

- Is the author a recognised authority on the subject?

Access

- Can I obtain a copy quickly and easily?

Currency

- How up to date is it?

Content

- Has it been peer-reviewed and, if not, can I trust it? (e.g. Could it be biased?)

- Does the abstract suggest that the content is relevant to my needs?

- Has any specialist terminology been adequately explained?

- Is the logic of the argument easy to follow?

- Does it discuss the findings of any new or interesting research?

Intended audience

- What is its intended audience? (e.g. Is it too specialist or too general for my purposes?)

Other printed sources can be evaluated by applying similar criteria and asking similar questions to establish their potential usefulness and significance.

Electronic sources

If your source is an electronic book or journal you may try adapting some of the questions that have been suggested for evaluating printed sources, while in the case of a website you may decide to ask:

Provenance

- What does the URL tell me about the reliability of the site? (e.g. Does it reside on the web server of an organisation that I can trust?)

- Who wrote the content?

Access

- Is the site readily accessible?

Currency

- When was it last updated?

Content

- Does it present any information that is unverifiable?

Intended audience

- Who is the website aimed at?

There are too many kinds of electronic information sources to include examples of each of them here. However, as you gain more experience of evaluating sources you will get better at determining your own criteria and devising your own resource-specific questions.

Oral sources

In the case of a lecture you may decide to ask:

Provenance

- Is the lecturer a recognised authority on the subject?

Content

- Does the lecturer draw upon first-hand experience or original research? If not, should I consult the sources the lecturer has used, rather than use the lecturer as a source?

- How does the lecturer's interpretation of the subject compare with that found in other sources?

- Have I correctly understood and accurately noted down what the lecturer has said?

In the case of an interview you may decide to ask:

Provenance

- Have I interviewed the right person to obtain the information I need?

Content

- Am I satisfied that the interviewee has fully understood my questions?

- Am I satisfied that the interviewee has responded truthfully to my questions?

- Have I accurately recorded what the interviewee has said?

- Have I done enough to anticipate and reduce the effects of bias (mine and the interviewee's)?

If you handle them well, interviews can produce a mine of information but if handled badly they can become a minefield. This complication arises because you choose the questions and record the answers. Thus you should take care in the way that you plan and conduct interviews, as well as in how you evaluate the information that you obtain from them.

Evaluating information: keeping it simple

You should keep the process of evaluating information as simple as possible, while still ensuring that you identify the most useful and significant sources that are available. Thus, you should not waste time in applying evaluation criteria or asking pertinent questions when this is unnecessary.

For example, when you are choosing texts from a recommended reading list there is no need to establish their provenance and currency since your tutors will already have done this. However, you should still evaluate the content of these sources as well as their accessibility in order to decide which are most likely to meet your information needs.

Such flexibility in your approach is not only logical and methodical. It is also efficient.

Using information: from evaluation to synthesis

After you have selected your sources you should identify the main ideas that are contained within them. When you have done this you can begin to explore the similarities and differences between these ideas to find out how they relate to each other. This is the key to understanding and using information since it enables you to make logical connections between the different ideas that you have identified in order to shape and support your own thinking.

Drawing upon other people's ideas in this way is a part of good scholarship and does not imply a lack of originality. It is the basis of what is called synthesis, which, in the context of university communication skills, Grellier and Goerke (2006, p. 158) describe as:

the pulling together of ideas from several sources into one coherent argument, which you can then present in writing or orally. The new product is your own argument.

That is, you can show originality in the way that you selectively use other people's ideas to produce your own new interpretation. This requires you to think critically in order to link together the main ideas that you have identified. You should not underestimate the importance of this skill; one of the most frequent criticisms of students' writing is that it is descriptive when it should be analytical. Thus, a good essay, for example, would present a synthesis of the main ideas that you have found rather than a simple descriptive summary of them.

Preparing a synthesis

A synthesis is often required in an essay argument, although you may also have to prepare a synthesis in the form of an oral discussion as your contribution to a seminar. However, the steps that you need to take to prepare a written or spoken synthesis are essentially the same and they can be summarised as follows.

1. Make sure that you clearly understand the assignment brief and consider how the nature of the task that you have been set will affect your choice of information sources and the criteria that you will use to evaluate them.

2. Identify the main idea(s) in each source that you have selected, as well as the evidence used to support them. Re-write these ideas in your own words (this is a good way of testing your understanding of what you have found).

3. Note any significant similarities or differences between these ideas and see how they relate to each other (e.g. Is there some common ground between them or are there only opposing views? Are they based on an interpretation of the same evidence and, if so, do they interpret it differently?).

4. Decide where you stand in relation to these ideas (e.g. What is your view in light of the information that you have found? Do you agree or disagree? Do you find one source more convincing than the others?). This is the key to creating your own argument, i.e. synthesis.

5. Now you can start to plan your response to the assignment task. Your plan should include a clear statement of your argument and set out the order in which you intend to critically discuss the ideas that you have identified.

Worked example

Using information from different sources to create a synthesis of the main ideas that you have identified

This example shows how you could go about preparing a synthesis of the main ideas found in four information sources, for an oral presentation. Please note that it is not the choice of sources or the synthesis itself that are important, but the process whereby the synthesis has been created. I have tried to make this process seem as straightforward as possible to show you that *using* information does not always have to be complicated or difficult.

The task

What is your response to the argument that separate special schooling is discriminatory and damaging to children with learning difficulties and disabilities (LDD)? Justify your point of view in an oral presentation lasting approximately 10 minutes.

1. Understanding the task in order to define your information needs

You would be expected to provide some convincing evidence to justify your response. Further, the education of children with LDD is a complex issue and you should take account of these complexities. A good response would, therefore, present a synthesis of main ideas that addressed separate special schooling from several different perspectives.

To illustrate how you might do this I have drawn upon the views of: the (former) Disability Rights Commission, Ofsted, the parents of young children with LDD, and a past president of the National Association of Head Teachers.

The evaluation criteria and questions that have been used are as follows:

Provenance

• Is the author a recognised authority on the subject?

• What is the significance of the document in relation to the debate on special schooling?

Access

• Can I obtain a copy of the document easily and quickly?

Currency

• How up to date is the information in the document?

Content

• How do the author's main ideas compare with those of others who have written about the subject?

Intended audience

• What is the intended audience?

The brevity of the selected criteria and questions reflect the nature of the task, i.e. it is a short presentation.

2. Identifying the main ideas in the selected information sources

The main ideas that were identified in the sources have been re-written, as follows:

Disability Rights Commission (2005) *Special Schools Debate – July 2005 Educational Opportunities for Disabled Children.*

Main ideas

- Full inclusion of all children with LDD in mainstream schools should be a long-term goal, to ensure equal citizenship.

- Parents should not be forced to choose special schools for their disabled children because of shortcomings in mainstream schools.

Ofsted (2006) *Inclusion: does it matter where pupils are taught?*

Main ideas

- The most important factor is not the type of school (special or mainstream) but the quality of education.

- There is more good provision for pupils with LDD in well resourced mainstream schools than in special schools.

Flewitt, R. and Nind, M. (2007) *Parents choosing to combine special and inclusive early years settings: the best of both worlds?*

Main ideas

- Many parents of young children with LDD opt for a combination of inclusive and special settings.

- Parents of young children with LDD do not regard inclusive education as *offering the best of both worlds in itself.*

Tutt, R. (2007) *Every child included.*

Main ideas

- Including more children with LDD in mainstream schools has worked well but this does not prove that it will work for every child with LDD.

- Treating inclusion as a human rights issue can deprive parents of choice.

3. Significant similarities and differences between the main ideas

Differences

- The DRC argues that all special schools should eventually be closed (i.e. the aim must be full inclusion).

- Tutt says that closing special schools would deprive parents of choice and that mainstream school placements may not be appropriate for some children with LDD.

- Ofsted regard inclusion as less important than the quality of the education that children with LDD receive.

- Flewitt and Nind found that some parents do not regard inclusion as the best option for their disabled children.

Similarities

- There is a consensus that inclusion can work well.

- Two sources identify the resourcing of mainstream provision as a major issue.

- Two sources consider parental choice to be an important right and this infers that they believe the option of special schooling should remain.

All four sources agree with the principle of inclusion but only the DRC advocates the closure of special schools (i.e. the ending of parental choice). In other words, the DRC appears to regard separate special schooling as 'discriminatory and damaging'.

4. Deciding where you stand in relation to these ideas

The following synthesis draws upon the main ideas that were identified in the four texts and illustrates how these ideas *could* be used to create a new argument. There is no *right* or *wrong* response. What matters is how well you justify your point of view.

- Separate special schooling is not, in itself, discriminatory or damaging to pupils with LDD. What is discriminatory and damaging is providing them with poor quality education and that happens in mainstream and special schools alike.

- Treating children with LDD as a group for whom only one form of schooling (i.e. inclusive education) is desirable misses the point. They are individuals and for some who are profoundly disabled, separate special schools may be more appropriate.

- There is also the matter of parental choice. In a democratic society we should respect the right of parents to choose the kind of schooling which they feel will best meet their children's special educational needs.

- However, parents should not be compelled to choose special schools because mainstream schools are making inadequate provision for children with LDD. Thus, real parental choice is likely to have significant funding implications.

- While the full inclusion of all children with LDD may seem to be a desirable social goal it is probably an unrealistic educational goal.

5. Planning your oral response to the task

Having prepared a synthesis (i.e. done the thinking) the next step is to plan the oral presentation.

Determining whether or not further information searching is required

It was stated at the beginning of the chapter that information searching is often an ongoing process. Thus, when you have prepared a synthesis of your findings it can be helpful to reflect upon what you have done and reconsider whether or not the outcome has fully satisfied your information needs.

For example, with reference to the presentation task, you may decide that your synthesis of main ideas should also take account of how pupils with LDD feel about special schools; in which case you would need some additional information. Alternatively, you may conclude that you have enough information and that no further searching is necessary. Such decisions are a matter of personal judgement and you should be prepared to make them.

Finally, if you use your information sources in this way you will be able to take control of them and demonstrate to your tutors that you can do your own thinking and arrive at your own conclusions, rather than submitting assignments that pass on other people's ideas but which contain few of your own.

Summary of key points

You are advised to evaluate every potential information source that you are thinking of using, to ensure that you select those that are most likely to meet your information needs.

Your evaluation must be logical and methodical, but you should be flexible in your choice of evaluation criteria and questions, in order to keep the process as simple as possible.

Once you have selected your information sources you should identify the main ideas that are contained in them and critically compare these ideas to see how they relate to each other. This will enable you to create a synthesis of your findings, which is the key to understanding and using information effectively.

References and further reading

You should find some of the following texts and websites helpful, especially when it comes to devising your own evaluation criteria.

Cornell University Library (2008) *Evaluating web sites: criteria and tools.* [online] Available at: **www.library.cornell.edu/olinuris/ref/research/webeval.html** This is a very user-friendly site with direct links to other web pages that provide advice on how to evaluate books and journal articles.

DCSF (2008) *The standards site: glossary of terms* [online] Available at: www.standards.dfes.gov.uk/thinkingskills/glossary/?view This site is intended for primary teachers and provides information on thinking skills programmes as well as a resource database and advice on how to develop children's thinking skills as part of curriculum delivery.

Disability Rights Commission (2005) *Special schools debate – July 2005 educational opportunities for disabled children.* [online] Available at: www.64.233.183.104/ search?q=cache:jpsrRKupJmkJ:valuingpeople.gov.uk/echo/

Flewitt, R. and Nind, M. (2007) Parents choosing to combine special and inclusive early years settings: the best of both worlds? *European Journal of Special Needs Education.* 22 (4) 425–41.

Grellier, J. and Goerke, V. (2006) *Communication skills toolkit: unlocking the secrets of tertiary success.* South Melbourne: Thomson Social Science Press. This book is particularly relevant to first year students and it offers ample and easy to follow advice on how to identify and evaluate information sources.

Ofsted (2006) *Inclusion: does it matter where pupils are taught?* [online] Available at: www.ofsted.gov.uk/publications/2535

QCA (2008) *National curriculum: creativity and critical thinking.* [online] Available at: http://curriculum.qca.org.uk/cross-curriculum-dimensions/creativitycritical thinking/ This site provides direct links to some useful resources for the development of creativity and critical thinking across the curriculum, from Early Years education to Key Stage 4.

Rumsey, S. (2004) *How to find information: a guide for researchers.* Maidenhead: Open University Press. As the title suggests, this book is aimed at those who are carrying out research (e.g. writing reports or dissertations). It offers much practical advice on the whole information seeking process, from planning your search to evaluating and managing your results.

Tutt, R. (2007) *Every child included.* London: Paul Chapman Publishing.

6. Presenting information in appropriate formats

Information literate students can effectively communicate the new knowledge and understanding that they have acquired.

Learning outcomes

Having worked through this chapter you should be better able to:

- **organise and present information in a variety of assignment formats;**

- **make effective use of the stylistic conventions that apply to these formats;**

- **understand and comply with the conventions that relate to confidentiality, anonymity and the ethical use of information.**

Informing others: being an effective communicator

It is not enough to be able to use information in order to help you to develop your own thinking and arrive at your own conclusions. If you are to do well on your course you must also be able to communicate what you have learnt in an appropriate format and style. Unless you are a budding literary genius and a gifted public speaker, this will require some careful thought and preparation.

A good place to start is by considering that your assignments will be amongst many that are competing for your tutor's attention and if they are poorly presented they are unlikely to be well-received. It helps, therefore, if you make your tutor's job a little easier by submitting text that follows the assignment guidelines and in which you convey your ideas in prose that is as clear, precise and error-free as possible. The same applies to oral presentations but these also require you to make good use of your voice and to engage with your audience. This may seem glaringly obvious but too many students ignore the obvious and consequently they fail to convey what they know in a way that meets the approval of their tutors. Since the assessment criteria that are used on your course will almost certainly include marks for *how* you present your assignments, it makes sense to abide by the common conventions that apply to coursework at university level.

While it may seem as though you can never please some tutors, that is no reason to give up trying; and if your work conveys the impression that you are not really trying, it will be marked accordingly.

Assignment formats

The three written assignment formats that are most widely used in higher education are the essay, report and dissertation. However, these are sometimes called other things. For example, you may be asked to prepare a report in the form of a child study or the evaluation of a school placement, and your tutor may refer to a dissertation as a thesis or long essay. These differences in terminology do not really matter provided that you have a clear understanding of your tutor's expectations as well as the conventions that apply to each type of format. Thus, for example, if your assignment brief does not specify whether your work should be set out in essay or report style, it is good information-seeking behaviour to ask your tutor for clarification before you begin writing.

You may also have to produce written coursework in other formats, such as learning journals and portfolios. What sets these forms of writing apart from essays, reports and dissertations (amongst other things) is that they are by their very nature personal and self-reflective, and they tend to be written over a much longer time-scale. There is also considerable variation between institutions regarding their design. That is, your tutor may advise you on how to format such documents or you may have to devise your own formats as part of the assessment criteria on your course. Further, electronic portfolios are becoming increasingly popular and numerous e-portfolio models are currently in use throughout the university sector (JISC, 2006, p. 2).

Therefore, the stylistic conventions that your tutors will expect you to observe when you are writing journals and portfolios are likely to be very course-specific and it is in your interests to ensure that you familiarise yourself with them and apply them accordingly.

Essays

The concise Oxford dictionary of literary terms defines the essay as:

> *a short written composition in prose that discusses a subject or proposes an argument without claiming to be a complete or thorough exposition.*
> (Baldick, 2001, p. 258)

In essays you will probably be expected to present an argument in which you respond to an assigned question, by declaring your point of view and supporting it with a reasoned discussion that is based on an evaluation of the available evidence (i.e. information).

The standard academic essay format is as follows.

Introduction – this indicates how you intend to answer the question, introduces the main points that will be discussed, says how your argument will be structured and informs the reader of the limits to your argument. In other words, the introduction tells your reader what to expect.

Main body – this consists of a series of paragraphs; each begins with a topic sentence denoting what is in the paragraph. Subsequent sentences develop the topic and each paragraph concludes with a sentence that links it to the next. This ensures that your argument flows smoothly from one paragraph to another.

Conclusion – this summarises the main points that you have discussed and reiterates how these have answered the essay question.

Reference list (*or bibliography*) – this provides full bibliographical details of all the sources that you have cited in the essay.

Reports

A report normally presents the findings of some form of investigation and is set out in separate sections, each with its own heading. While there are many different kinds of report and, therefore, considerable variation in how they are structured, the following format is widely used.

Title page – in addition to the title of the report, the date, and your name, you will probably be expected to include details of your course.

Contents page – unlike essays, reports usually have a contents page.

Summary – like the abstract for a dissertation, this brief informative statement tells the reader what is in your report.

Introduction – this briefly describes the background to your report, its scope and limitations, and its intended purpose.

Main body – in long reports the main body is divided into sections and sub-sections, each focused on a particular topic (or sub-topic) and each with its own heading (or sub-heading).

Conclusions – the discussion in the main body should arrive at a number of conclusions and these must be presented and explained in an ordered sequence.

Recommendations – not all reports result in recommendations but if these are made you can present them along with your conclusions (i.e. in a 'conclusions and recommendations' section) or in a separate section, immediately after the conclusions.

Appendices – any detailed material that interferes with the main flow of your discussion should be included in an appendix (in some reports an appendix is called an annex).

Reference list (or bibliography) – as with essays, you must provide details of the information sources that you have used.

You may be expected to number the sections and sub-sections of your reports (e.g. 1. Introduction) but even if you are not, this can be a very helpful way of guiding your reader through the text.

Occasionally tutors blur the distinction between essays and reports, and ask students to use headings in some of their essays; hence you need to read carefully every assignment brief and follow your tutor's instructions.

Dissertations

Seely (1998, p. 76) states that 'in essence, a dissertation is an extended essay'. Further, they are referred to as research reports on some courses. In light of having distinguished between essays, reports and dissertations, this may seem a little confusing. However, what matters is not the names that are used to describe the assignments that you write, but the formats in which you present them for assessment.

In addition to a title page, contents page and abstract, dissertations are usually formatted in sections (e.g. chapters) similar to the following.

Introduction – this outlines the aims, methods and results of your research.

Literature review – this discusses critically the significant information that you have identified in the sources that you have selected, and sets the scene for your own research.

Scope and aims of the research – this explains the purpose of your research and defines its limitations.

Research methods – this provides a rationale for your choice of methods and describes how you carried out your investigation.

Research findings – this presents your research data, mainly in the form of tables and figures.

An interpretation of the findings – this explains the significance of what you have found, along with any implications for the improvement of educational practice.

Summary and conclusions – the main conclusions that you have reached are summarised and the implications for future research are noted.

Appendices and reference list (or bibliography) – as with reports, these complete the dissertation.

Reflective task

What does a good report look like?

Report writing is more direct and to the point than essay writing, since reports are meant to provide information rather than persuade by argument. The introduction and conclusion to *Ethnicity and degree attainment*, a report prepared for the DfES by Broecke and Nicholls (2007), demonstrate this businesslike style.

It may be helpful to read these two sections of the document (they are very brief) to see how they compare with your own approach to report writing and formatting. You may also wish to consider what it is about the authors' writing style and the physical layout of their report that make it so easy for you to take in the information that they have presented.

The report can be quickly accessed online, by using one of the major search engines and typing in 'Ethnicity and degree attainment'; or by going to the Department for Children, Schools and Families website and entering 'Ethnicity and degree attainment' in the search box. After you have read the introduction and conclusion, compare your reflections with the comments made below.

Reports have to look attractive on the page if they are to capture and maintain the reader's attention. This means that they must be easy on the eye, with plenty of white space to break up the text and good use of graphic signposts to guide the reader along. They should be written in plain English, unless they are intended for a specialist audience, and excessively long and complicated sentences should be avoided.

Journals and portfolios

These two assignment formats will be discussed together because they are the most problematic when it comes to offering advice on how to use them in order to organise and present information. That is, as has already been noted, the stylistic conventions that are applied to them vary greatly between universities.

A reflective learning journal is a systematic way of maintaining a record of learning experiences and your reflections upon them. On some programmes they are a separate and significant item of assessed coursework, while on others they form a component part of a larger assignment. Further, the terms learning journal and learning diary are sometimes used interchangeably (like extended essay and dissertation) and sometimes used to denote two different things. Thus, some tutors regard learning diaries as confidential documents in which students record their private thoughts, and such diaries are not intended to be submitted for assessment. It goes without saying that this use of terminology can be a little confusing,

However, learning journals are meant to support reflective practice and despite wide variation in terms of how they are formatted and the media in which they are recorded, they are all likely to include the following basic elements.

- Descriptions of significant events and experiences.

- Reflections on these events and experiences.

- A record of actions taken as a result of personal reflection.

- Evidence of course-related reading.

If you have to devise your own learning journal format you should find out what your tutors expect in terms of the medium to be used (e.g. a written or electronic record) and the content (e.g. the balance between descriptive and reflective writing). This will provide you with a starting point and if the journal really is to be a record of *your* learning development, the rest is down to you.

The term portfolio is less likely to cause confusion than 'learning journal', although a portfolio can be an assessed piece of coursework (i.e. a task set by your tutor); or a professional development portfolio, which you may want to use in order to obtain accreditation of prior learning and achievement before you enrol at university (QAA, 2004, p. 12).

As coursework, portfolios can be single modular assignments that are undertaken as alternatives to essays; or they may be much larger documents that are divided into sections and which contain a wide range of evidence of learning activity, such as essays, school observations, and lesson plans. If you have to produce a portfolio you should ask your tutor for clear and specific guidance on what to include in it and how it should be formatted.

A professional development portfolio (PDP) or professional development record, as it is also called, is a confidential collection of material that records and reflects your work (DfES, 2001, p. 1). Unlike a course portfolio, it is meant to be maintained throughout your working life, and all decisions regarding its content and format are your responsibility. Some very practical advice on how to prepare one can be found in the DfES document *Helping you develop: guidance on producing a professional development record.* (You can quickly access a copy by using any of the major internet search engines and typing in the document's title.)

If you intend to use a PDP to obtain accreditation of prior learning and achievement you should give appropriate emphasis to those aspects of your experience which best support your application.

Presentations

The key to a good presentation lies in careful and intelligent preparation. Like essays and reports, presentations need a clear structure, that is, an introduction, a main body and conclusion. It may be difficult to avoid using PowerPoint as your medium if 'the effective use of technology' is one of the marking criteria for the assignment.

Your introduction should be welcoming and include a brief explanation of the content and purpose of the presentation. As well as good eye contact, a smile and a pleasant tone of voice, it can also help if you include a slide that grabs the attention of your audience while still remaining within the bounds of public decency.

The main points that you intend to discuss should be set out in a logical sequence and this will largely be determined by the content of the presentation itself. However, you are advised to 'move from the known to the unknown, and from the easy to the difficult' (Seely, 1998, p. 55). In other words, you should present your main points in a way that allows the audience to take them in *gradually* (i.e. in stages), rather than risk overwhelming them with too much information.

It goes without saying that any text or images that you intend to use should be clearly visible to every member of the audience. The best way to ensure this is to see for yourself what your slides will look like from the back of the room in which you will deliver the presentation.

As with an essay or report, try to conclude with a summing up that leaves your audience with a favourable impression. This is easier said than done but you will only receive a good mark for the assignment if you impress your tutor. If you are expected to allow the audience to ask questions it is usually best to leave this until the end, but to make this clear during your introduction.

Finally, handouts can be a useful way of providing your audience with any detailed background information that cannot be incorporated into the presentation itself. If you do provide handouts you must ensure that there are enough to go around and that they are easy to read.

Stylistic conventions

In order to improve your academic writing you must be prepared to acquire good habits and avoid bad ones. One good habit is to check each assignment, prior to its submission, to ensure that your work is consistent with the writing conventions that apply at university level. This sounds straightforward but you have probably learnt already that some things at university are not always straightforward.

For example, it is a common convention that block quotations must be indented and single-spaced. However, there is no generally agreed definition of what constitutes a block quotation. Thus, on some courses students are advised to indent and single-space any quotation that is longer than one line of typed text, while on others they are told that they should only do so if the quotation is two sentences or longer.

In other words, although there are common conventions that govern academic writing, there is also considerable variation in how some of these are applied at different universities, and on different courses within the same universities. It is, therefore, in your interests to find out what some of these common conventions are and how your course team interprets them. This means that you should be proactive (another good habit) and accept that it is your responsibility to learn the rules of the writing game, rather than remain inactive and wait to be told where you have gone wrong when you receive your marking feedback.

It is not possible to discuss every academic writing convention here since there are far too many of them. For example, the British edition of *A manual for writers of research papers, theses and dissertations* (Turabian, 1982) contains a 14-page section on how to format quotations; while *Fowler's modern English usage* runs to more than 800 pages of advice on grammar, syntax, and style. Therefore, the following guidance provides no more than a brief overview of what your tutors are likely to expect, and you are reminded that it is your responsibility to ensure that your writing style is consistent with their expectations.

Citations and referencing

The Harvard (or author-date) referencing system is the most widely used in higher education and it is very likely the one that your course team has adopted. (As you will have noticed, it is also the one that is used throughout this book.) While it is a system, there are some minor stylistic variations in how it is interpreted at different universities.

Your institution or your course team should provide you with a copy of the referencing guidelines that you will be expected to follow. Whatever these are, you must correctly reference all direct quotations and paraphrases that are included in your assignments. Unless you do this you may be accused of plagiarism, even if it is unintended.

When you cite a published source in the main body of an assignment you must normally provide the author's surname, the year of publication and the relevant page number. (There are a few exceptions to this rule. For example, it is accepted practice not to include the authors of standard reference works, such as dictionaries and atlases, but to cite the names of the texts instead.)

In your reference list (or bibliography) you must provide additional details, including the author's initials, the name of the publisher and the place of publication. Again, this sounds straightforward but far too many students hand in work that has been incorrectly referenced. This is often because they get these additional details wrong or because, when they are citing less commonly used sources (such as conference papers and online discussion lists), they are unsure of what details to include.

Practical task

Identifying the conventions that apply to referencing

It is better to be safe than sorry when it comes to referencing, especially when you use sources where the details of authorship and publication are not clear-cut. This task is intended to draw your attention to some of the challenges that can arise when you are referencing such material.

Depending on the nature of the guidance that your institution provides, you may need to consult some additional referencing sources in order to complete the task. However, this should not be too difficult since many universities make their referencing guidelines available on the internet, and some are very comprehensive.

Practical task continued

The task is to find out how to reference:

- a book published in a new edition;

- a book with more than four authors;

- a chapter of a book that has been complied by an editor but in which the individual chapters have been written by different authors;

- an Act of Parliament (e.g. the Education Reform Act 1988);

- another student's dissertation (i.e. an unpublished source);

- a text that is undated;

- a text that has no named author;

- an electronic journal article;

- a book that is available on an online platform;

- an interview that has been broadcast on television.

Quotations and paraphrases

A paraphrase is the reworking of a passage that conveys its original meaning but in your own words. Do not be tempted to think that if you change a few words you can pass off someone else's ideas as your own; all universities impose very serious penalties for doing this.

Paraphrases can be very useful alternatives to quotations. That is, you should avoid excessive use of quotations since this looks unattractive on the page and conveys the impression that *you* have nothing important to say.

Worked example

A quotation and paraphrase

In *Doing your research project* Bell (2005, p.10) states that:

> *the case study approach can be particularly appropriate for individual researchers because it provides an opportunity for an aspect of a problem to be studied in some depth.*

Note that this is a block quotation so that a colon precedes it, the text is indented, and no quotation marks are used.

If you were to rework this passage (for example) as

> *a case study approach is very appropriate when researchers are working on their own because it gives them a chance to examine a particular problem in some detail* (italics have been used for emphasis)

then you should acknowledge its original source. That is, you should indicate where the idea came from, by referencing it, even though you have expressed the idea in your own words.

Print enhancements

As with quotations, if you make excessive use of print enhancements your work will look less attractive. This is a matter of personal judgement but most tutors do not appreciate being confronted with assignments that are characterised by a bewildering variety of font sizes and types, underlining, bold text, capital letters and italics. Print enhancements may get your work noticed, but for the wrong reasons.

Abbreviations and contractions

An abbreviation is made up of one or more letters of a full word or term, thus Mr and BBC are abbreviations. In many cases points are not included (note that Mr is used rather than Mr.) but in others they are, so that in a reference list, for instance, Cm. (rather than Cm) may be used to indicate that the text is a Command Paper.

A contraction consists of one or more words that have been shortened but it retains the final letter of the original word or words. Therefore, o'clock and can't are contractions rather than abbreviations. While the first is a rare example of a contraction that is accepted in academic writing (i.e. it is now very unusual to see 'of the clock' in print) the second, like most contractions, is unacceptable.

However, if you are directly quoting an information source in which a contraction has been used, you must include that contraction in your quotation. Further, if you are keeping a reflective learning journal or diary your tutor may allow you to use contractions, since journal and diary writing are less formal than essay and report writing.

Dealing with abbreviations is more complicated since, unlike contractions, many are commonly used in academic writing. Thus, GCSE, MA, Dr, et al., and Unesco are accepted forms; but gym, dept., chap., Sept., and Prof. are not (except perhaps in journal and diary writing). As these examples also illustrate, abbreviations can be a mix of upper and lower case letters, and some include points while others have none. Consequently, finding out which abbreviations are acceptable and how to format them will require time and effort. A good place to begin (if you have not already done so) is to ask your tutor for any course-specific guidelines and to check out your institution's library catalogue to see if a dictionary of abbreviations is available.

Numbers

It is common practice to spell out numbers under ten, for example, you should use 'nine' rather than '9'. However, there are some exceptions to this rule. For example, when you are providing measurements numbers under 10 should be expressed as figures (e.g. 6mm and 8%) but you should never begin a sentence with a numerical figure, no matter how large. Thus, do not begin a sentence with:

> *750 pupils are enrolled at the school* . . . but use *Seven hundred and fifty pupils are enrolled at the school* . . . or, even better, rephrase the sentence and say *There are 750 pupils enrolled at the school* . . .

Very large numbers are commonly expressed in figures and units of millions and billions, thus, for example, use 7 billion rather than 7, 0000, 0000, 000.

Punctuation

There is very little excuse for submitting work in which there are numerous errors in punctuation, since it suggests that you do not know how to use the appropriate computer software to correct them, or that you are unprepared to make the effort.

If punctuation is a more serious problem you may try writing in shorter sentences, since these reduce the likelihood of error. This does not mean that your style need be any less 'academic'. Good writing is characterised by simplicity and directness, not by long-winded phrases and meandering sentences.

However, while you can reduce punctuation you cannot avoid it, and one virtually unavoidable punctuation mark is the apostrophe. Its two basic purposes are to indicate missing letters (as in *o'clock*) and to show possession (as in *the pupil's report*).

Thus *1990's* is incorrect since the apostrophe neither indicates the omission of a letter or possession (*1990s* is correct).

The apostrophe can be confusing when used with words ending in *s*. A simple rule to remember is that when a singular words ends with *s*, you show possession by adding an *'s*; and when a plural word ends with *s*, you add an apostrophe to show possession.

Thus, *the class's results were very good* is correct (not *the class' results*) and *the boys' school* is correct (not *the boys's school*).

Quotation marks (or inverted commas) are used for short quotations, emphasis and for direct speech, though in a piece of academic writing you would be more concerned with the first two. UK style favours single quotes with doubles for a quotation or something which needs emphasis within the quotation. US style favours the opposite: double quotes with singles within.

Personal pronouns

It is unlikely that your tutors will wish you to make much use of personal pronouns (e.g. *I, you,* and *me*) in any of your writing, with the possible exception of reflective learning journals and diaries.

Thus, for example, in a report you should not say *I carried out a survey* . . . but use *The writer carried out a survey* . . . or, even better, make your style impersonal and use *A survey was carried out.*

Finally, since it is better to avoid mistakes than to learn from them, you are advised to use your information skills in order to find out how your course team interpret the common stylistic conventions of academic writing, and to ensure that you observe these conventions in your own writing.

Confidentiality and anonymity

Your institution will have policy guidelines on confidentiality and anonymity, and you must comply with these when you are handling information. Put simply, you should not inform anyone else of something that has been said in confidence, without the consent of the person who has said it. Thus, if you were on a school placement and a pupil's father informed you, in confidence, that he thought the class teacher was incompetent, it would be unethical for you to tell anyone else, even if it was true.

Anonymity is different from confidentiality in that anonymous information can be passed on to others, provided that you do not reveal its source. There are simple ways of doing this in your assignments, such as referring to a pupil as *Pupil A*, rather than using his or her real name; or referring to a school as *the placement school.*

However, you should be careful that you do not inadvertently reveal the name of a person or institution that must be kept anonymous, by naming that person or institution in your reference list. For example, there is little point in maintaining a school's anonymity throughout an 8000 word research paper if you include the school's Ofsted report in your reference list and, thereby, name the school.

Complying with intellectual property and copyright conventions

Copyright laws extend to digital as well as printed material and everyone in higher education is bound by them. These laws govern your right to reproduce information that you have obtained from any intellectual work that is subject to copyright, such as: books, newspapers, music, films, photographs, maps, computer software and websites.

The agreement that your institution has reached with the Copyright Licensing Agency will determine what you can copy, as well as the terms and conditions that apply. For example, it may be legal to make a single copy of a journal article but not to make multiple copies to use as a handout when you deliver a presentation. Since a criminal prosecution can result from the infringement of copyright laws you should always observe the copyright restrictions that apply at your institution.

Plagiarism

The shorter Oxford English dictionary (1983) defines plagiarism as 'the taking and using as one's own of the thoughts, writings or inventions of another'. (Note that this definition has been presented within quotation marks and that the original source has been acknowledged.)

All colleges and universities forbid plagiarism, whether it is intentional or accidental, and the punishment for it can be severe. Thus, like infringing copyright, it is not worth risking. The best way to avoid being suspected of plagiarism is to ensure that whenever you quote or paraphrase someone else's words or ideas that you cite and refer to the original source.

Please note that this advice applies equally to oral presentations and written coursework. Hopefully it will not put you off your studies but, instead, encourage you to be an ethical user of information.

Summary of key points

There are some important differences in the way that your tutors will expect you to format different types of assignment (e.g. essays, reports and learning journals). You should ensure that you have a clear understanding of these differences and format your work accordingly.

Numerous stylistic conventions are applied to academic writing and there is considerable variation in how they are interpreted throughout the university sector. It is in your interests to make yourself aware of these conventions and to find out how your tutors have interpreted them.

Information must be handled ethically. Therefore you must always follow your institution's policy guidelines in relation to confidentiality and anonymity.

Further, you must not infringe copyright laws or plagiarise the work of others. If you do, the risks are great and the punishments can be severe.

References and further reading

University and college libraries abound with texts that offer detailed guidance on how to format coursework, and the choice can seem bewildering. However, if you have clearly defined your information needs beforehand, selecting an appropriate text should not be too difficult.

Baldick, C. (2001) *The concise Oxford dictionary of literary terms.* Oxford: Oxford University Press.

Bell, J. (2005) *Doing your research project: a guide for first-time researchers in education, health and social science.* 4th edition. Maidenhead: Open University Press.

Broecke, S. and Nicholls, T. (2007) *Ethnicity and degree attainment.* London: Department for Education and Skills. [online] Available at: **www.dcsf.gov.uk/research/data/uploadfiles/RW92.pdf**

Burchfield, R.W. (2004) *Fowler's modern English usage.* 3rd edition. Oxford: Oxford University Press.

DfES (2001) *Helping you develop: guidance on producing a professional development record.* Nottingham: DfES Publications. [online] Available at: **www.teachernet.gov.uk/_doc/840/Text-Help_to_Dev_T.pdf** While it is aimed at teachers, the guidance in this document is useful for anyone working in education who wishes to produce or update a professional development portfolio.

JISC (2006) *e-portfolios introduction.* London: Joint Information Systems Committee [online] Available at: **www.jiscinfonet.ac.uk/InfoKits/effective-use-of-VLEs/e-portfolios** This document explains what an e-portfolio is and provides an overview of several models of e-portfolios that are currently in use in higher education institutions.

QAA (2004) *Guidelines for the accreditation of prior learning.* London: Quality Assurance Agency for Higher Education. [online] Available at: **www.qaa.ac.uk/academicinfrastructure/apl/default.asp**

Seely, J. (1998) *The Oxford guide to writing and speaking.* Oxford: Oxford University Press. The book includes some useful advice on presentations and assignment writing, and a very informative and user-friendly section on paragraphing. A new and slightly expanded edition called *The Oxford guide to effective writing and speaking* is also available.

The shorter Oxford English dictionary (1983). 3rd revised edition. Oxford: Oxford University Press.

Turabian, K.L. (1982) *A manual for writers of research papers, theses and dissertations.* Revised British Edition. London: William Heinemann.

7. Self-assessment and self-reflection

Many aspects should be considered in information literacy assessment, and it is virtually impossible to develop an instrument that will address them all adequately.
(Neely, 2006, p. 162)

Learning outcomes

Having worked through this chapter you should be better able to:

- **understand the purposes and nature of information skills assessment;**

- **assess your current level of information skills competence;**

- **decide what to do in response to your self-assessment outcome.**

How information literate do you need to be?

This question is very hard to answer. Your course-related information needs will determine the skills that you must apply and the level to which you must apply them. Therefore, one criterion against which you can measure your current information skills competence is the extent to which you are able to satisfy these needs, i.e. achieve a satisfactory standard in your coursework. However, it is not the only criterion and if you wish to do well on your course you must not allow yourself to be too easily satisfied. From defining your information needs to presenting information in appropriate formats, the greater the level of skill that you acquire the better you will be at coping with the information demands that arise from your course, and the better prepared you will become for the information demands of the real world that exists beyond higher education.

How information literate you wish to be is a matter of personal choice but you should bear in mind that what constitutes a satisfactory standard in any context will change over time (Catts and Lau, 2008, p. 29). In other words, if you are to maintain an appropriate level of information competence you must be prepared to go on developing your skills in response to further technological change and the inevitable advent of new sources and forms of information. Ideally you will be a self-motivated and autonomous learner who actively engages with a wide variety of information sources. This will sharpen your critical thinking skills and help you to become more adept at asking the sorts of informed questions that will enable you to use information in order to construct your own understanding. In turn, this should give you greater confidence when it comes to making your own professional judgements and challenging expert educational opinion when you *think* that it is wrong. Such a capacity for informed self-reflection lies at the heart of the concept of being a graduate. It also marks the essential difference between being a *passive* or *active* learner, and it underpins the very notion of self-directed and lifelong learning.

Information skills assessment in higher education

Comparatively little developmental work on information skills assessment for university students has been undertaken and most of it has been carried out in the United States and Australia. Nonetheless, a considerable number of information skills assessment instruments have been devised by staff at individual institutions. Neely (2006, p. 158), for example, identified and reviewed over 70 that were in use in American universities; the majority of which have been posted on the Web rather than published. Thus you can easily carry out your own information search to obtain an overview of the range of these skills tests, including some that have been prepared by librarians and academic staff at British universities.

In addition to these institution-based assessments, three standardised *information literacy surveys* have also been developed for use at national level in American and Australian universities. These are: the Standardized Assessment of Information Literacy Skills (SAILS), the iSkills Test, and the Information Skills Survey (ISS). If you are interested in finding out more about them you are advised to begin your search with Catts and Lau (2008, p. 20). Their report on *Information literacy indicators* is concise and very readable, and it can be accessed online. (The URL can be found in the reference list at the end of this chapter.)

The assessment task that is set out below, and which follows on from the one in the first chapter, is not an alternative to any institutional assessment that you may be expected to undertake. Nor is it in any sense standardised; it is meant to be self-administered, self-interpreted and carried out over any timescale that you feel is appropriate. Its main purpose is to encourage you to reflect upon how you go about the process of seeking, accessing, evaluating and presenting information. Therefore, the answers that you provide to the questions are far less important than what you may decide to do in response to any skills deficits that you identify.

Whatever your decision, you should be realistic and set yourself achievable goals rather than trying to do too much at once. You should also remember that the skills that you are developing in order to cope with the information demands of your course are the same skills that will need in order to cope with the information demands that will be made upon you throughout your working life.

Self-assessment task

1. Recognising the need for information

Defining your needs

- Assignment briefs frequently include such process words as *analyse*, *compare*, *discuss*, and *evaluate*. Do you understand the differences between such terms when they are applied to academic writing? For example, are you aware of how *discussion* differs from *evaluation*?

- Do you use the key terminology in your assignment briefs to narrow down the definition of your information needs as much as possible, before you begin to search for information?

- When deciding where to start looking for information do you first weigh up the relative merits of oral, printed and electronic sources, or are you mainly reliant on internet searching?

- If you are unsure about what you are being asked to do in an assignment brief do you know whom to ask for help or advice?

The value and relevance of potential sources

- Do you know what makes some information sources more authoritative than others?

- Are you confident that you can detect bias in information sources?

- How do you establish whether or not an author is an acknowledged authority?

- How do you decide whether or not an educational publisher is reputable?

Constraints that may affect your search

- Are you aware of the range of education-related information sources that your institution makes available and do you know how to access them?

- Are you aware of the range of education-related information sources that other institutions (e.g. the British Library) make available and do you know how to access them?

- Are you aware of the range of education-related information sources that are available online and do you know how to access them?

- Do you plan your information searches to take account of the ease and speed with which you can locate and access sources?

- If you are unsure about the range of information sources that your institution makes available do you know whom to ask for help or advice?

Reassessing your needs

- Do you reassess your information needs in light of your initial search results?

- Do you manage your search time efficiently and do you know *when* it is time to stop looking for more information?

2. Information seeking strategies

Selecting methods and tools

- Are you confident in your ability to choose the most appropriate method(s) when you are searching for information?

- Are you confident in your ability to choose the most appropriate tool(s) when you are searching for information?

- If you are having difficulty with an information search do you know whom to ask for help or advice?

Formulating and executing a search strategy

- How effective are you at planning a search strategy?

- How effective are you at carrying out a search strategy?

Using selected methods and tools to find information

- Do you make effective use of the search methods you employ?

- Do you make effective use of the search tools that you employ?

3. Locating and accessing information

The range of sources

- Do you know how to locate and access the main education-related information sources that are available in print?

- Do you know how to locate and access the main education-related information sources that are available online?

- Do you know how to locate and access oral sources of information?

- If you are unsure about how to locate and access any of these sources do you know whom to ask for help or advice?

Searching effectively

- Are you able to carry out an effective information search in a library?

- Are you able to carry out an effective information search using the internet?

- Whether it is available in printed or electronic form, are you effective at locating the information that you need in the texts that you have selected?

4. Evaluating information

The usefulness and significance of information

- Are you aware of and are you able to apply appropriate evaluation criteria to printed sources?

- Are you aware of and are you able to apply appropriate evaluation criteria to electronic sources?

- Are you aware of and are you able to apply appropriate evaluation criteria to oral sources?

Using different sources to create a synthesis

- Do you find it easy to identify the main ideas in your information sources?

- Are you able to draw upon the main ideas from different information sources in order to shape and support your own thinking?

- Are you effective at using the main ideas that you have found in your sources to create your own argument (i.e. synthesis)?

Reassessing your needs

- Do you reflect upon your findings to consider whether or not the outcome of your search has fully met your information needs?

- What do you do if you decide that your information needs have not been fully met?

5. Presenting information in appropriate formats

Written assignments

- Are you competent at presenting work in a report format?

- Are you competent at presenting work in an essay format?

- Are you competent at presenting work in a dissertation format?

- If you are required to present written work in other formats (e.g. teaching practice file or portfolio) do you feel that you can deal with them competently?

Oral presentations

- Do you know how to put together and deliver an effective oral presentation?

- Are you able to make effective use of the relevant ICT (e.g. PowerPoint) in order to deliver effective oral presentations?

- If you are unsure about how to use any of the relevant ICT do you know where you can seek appropriate help and advice (e.g. from printed sources, online sources and relevant staff within your institution)?

Stylistic conventions

- Are you aware of the common stylistic conventions that apply to each of the formats in which you are required to produce written coursework (e.g. citation and referencing, quotations and paraphrases, and the use of personal pronouns)?

- Are you aware of the particular stylistic conventions that your institution applies to each of the formats in which you are required to produce written coursework (e.g. citation and paraphrasing, quotations, and the use of personal pronouns)?

- If you are unsure about any of these stylistic conventions do you know where you can seek appropriate help and advice (e.g. from printed sources, online sources and relevant staff within your institution)?

Confidentiality and anonymity

- Are you aware of the difference between confidentiality and anonymity?

- Are you aware of your institution's policy guidelines on confidentiality and anonymity, and do you consciously observe these guidelines when you are communicating information?

- If you are unsure about these policy guidelines do you know whom to ask for help or advice?

Intellectual property and copyright

- Are you aware of the terms and conditions that apply to your institution's arrangements with the Copyright Licensing Agency?

- If you are unsure about these terms and conditions do you know whom to ask for help or advice?

- Are you aware of the penalties that can be imposed if you break copyright law?

Plagiarism

- Do you understand what plagiarism is and are you aware of your own institution's guidelines on how to avoid plagiarism?

- If you are unsure about these guidelines do you know whom to ask for help or advice?

- Are you aware of the penalties that your institution may impose if you are found to have plagiarised the work of others?

Reflecting upon the outcome of your self-assessment

All students in higher education are encouraged to be self-reflective and this ability to critically think about and learn from your own experience is essential if you are to become more information literate. The comments which follow are intended to help you in the process of reflecting upon the outcome of the assessment task and include some suggestions about what you may do if you are concerned about your current level of information literacy. However, ultimate responsibility for the development of your information skills rests with you. No one else can do your thinking for you and unless you engage in some purposeful self-reflection you are unlikely to enhance your information skills.

1. Recognising the need for information

Defining your needs

It is easy to misunderstand an assignment brief and define your information needs incorrectly; therefore it pays to carefully read each brief. If you are unsure about what you have been asked to do you should seek clarification from the tutor who set the assignment.

If you are having problems with assignment briefs in general it may be better to request help from your institution's learning support service.

The value and relevance of potential information sources

Most tutors will expect you to use a combination of printed and electronic texts and if you have problems with locating and accessing any of these you should seek help in your institution's library. The appropriate librarian will also be able to advise you on how to restrict your information choices to authoritative sources.

Constraints that may affect your search

You must not allow yourself to spend too much time searching for information. Therefore it pays to find out what range of authoritative and education-related sources is available in your institution's library and online, and how to access them.

Reassessing your needs

Only you can decide when you have enough information with which to complete an assignment. If you have a set reading list this should be straightforward but if not, and you are in doubt, you should seek guidance from your tutor.

2. Information seeking strategies

Selecting methods and tools

Your choice of search methods and tools will vary according to the nature of your assignments. If you are in doubt about which tools or methods are the most appropriate for any information search you should visit your institution's library and ask for help.

Formulating and executing a search strategy

Having a strategy is preferable to random information searching and it will save you time if you choose the most appropriate search terms before you begin. If you are unsure about your strategy you should ask a librarian for help.

Using selected methods and tools to find information

Do not be afraid to use a particular method or tool because you are unfamiliar with it. In the event that you do not find the information that you are seeking within reasonable time you should ask a librarian for advice. It may be that you are using your methods and tools ineffectively or that you have selected the wrong ones.

3. Locating and accessing information

The range of sources

Some students tend to over-use electronic sources and this may give their tutors the impression that they are avoiding the library. Since course teams usually attach great importance to the book and journal collections that they ask their libraries to purchase, failure to make appropriate use of them is unwise.

If you are unsure about how to make effective use of oral sources (e.g. to plan and conduct interviews) you will probably find some useful guidance in your institution's library.

Searching effectively

Being effective means finding the information that you need in whatever source it is located. It is not the same as being efficient but ideally you will be able to combine the two. Your institution's librarians can help you with any problems that you may have in using indexes and databases, and the learning support staff should be able to advise you on such techniques as skimming and scanning text if you are having difficulties in extracting information from the sources that you have identified.

4. Evaluating information

The usefulness and significance of information

The guidance provided in Chapter 5 should help you to decide which evaluation criteria to apply to the information sources that you identify. Such evaluation is a part of good scholarship and it will help you to narrow down your choice of sources to those that are the most significant.

Using different sources to create a synthesis

There is no quick and easy way to go about identifying and comparing the main ideas that you find in different information sources in order to create your own synthesis of them. As the worked example in Chapter 5 shows, the process can be broken down into several stages and if you are having difficulty with any of these you should seek advice from your institution's learning support service.

Reassessing your needs

It is always useful to reconsider whether or not your information needs have been met before you submit your work for assessment.

5. Presenting information in appropriate formats

Written assignments

If you fail to present your work in the required format you are likely to be penalised. It can be helpful to look at some examples of other students' writing (e.g. reports and dissertations) to gain a better sense of how to format your own. You may wish to ask your tutor or a librarian if this is possible.

Oral presentations

A presentation is a kind of performance and good performances are well planned and well rehearsed; they do happen spontaneously. You should practise your delivery before the big day and if this can be done in co-operation with other students, all the better.

Stylistic conventions

Your tutors will regard some stylistic conventions (e.g. punctuation, citation and referencing) as more important than others and you should ensure that you submit work that is consistent with their expectations. You should also try to format your text so that it looks attractive on the page; i.e. appearances count.

Confidentiality and anonymity

It is your responsibility to follow your institution's regulations on confidentiality and anonymity, so it pays to read them carefully and make sure that you understand them. If you intend to work in education you should be able to demonstrate to your tutors that you know how to handle confidential information.

Intellectual property and copyright

If you are in doubt about your institution's copyright licensing agreement you should ask one of your librarians for guidance. Any serious infringement of copyright law can have serious consequences and it is better to be safe than sorry.

Plagiarism

Even though it may be unintentional, if you use the words or ideas of someone else without attributing their original source, you will have committed plagiarism. It is your responsibility to ensure that you understand and follow your institution's guidelines on referencing and citation.

Some final thoughts on self-help

Your assignment feedback will tell you a great deal about any shortcomings that you may have in the way that you select and make use of information. It is foolish to ignore such comments, just as it is foolish to ignore the many sources of help and advice that your institution makes available. Godwin (2006, p. 270), who is a university librarian, notes the reluctance of many students to consult academic librarians and their preference to navigate the web by trial and error, rather than to follow the advice that is provided in their institution's manuals and help sheets. DIY solutions are sometimes expedient but they are not the solution to every information problem that may arise. Librarians have expert knowledge, that is, they are also a valuable source of information. If you fail to make effective use of them during your time in higher education you will have much to lose and only yourself to blame.

Summary of key points

Your course-related information needs will determine the skills that you must apply and the level to which you must apply them. However, you should ensure that you do not underestimate these needs.

In order to maintain an appropriate level of information competence you must be prepared to go on developing your skills in response to further technological change and the advent of new sources and forms of information.

Self-assessment can help you to identify any information skills deficits that you have but if it is to be effective you must do it thoughtfully so as to avoid overrating or underrating your ability.

If you identify any information skills deficits you must be realistic in deciding what to do about them and, where appropriate, you should seek help or advice from the relevant staff in your institution.

References and further reading

These documents provide some interesting insights into the various methods of assessing information skills that are currently in use.

Catts, R. and Lau, J. (2008) *Towards information literacy indicators.* Paris: Unesco. [online] Available at: **www.uis.unesco.org/template/pdf/cscl/InfoLit.pdf** The authors present a persuasive case for the development of information literacy on an international level and their framework includes brief sections on higher education and information literacy criteria for teachers.

Godwin, P. (2006) Information literacy in the age of amateurs: how Google and Web 2.0 affect librarians' support of information literacy. *eLit* 5 (4): 268–87. [online] Available at: **www.ics.heacademy.ac.uk/italics/vol5iss4.htm**

Neely, T.Y. (2006) *Information literacy assessment: standards-based tools and assignments.* Chicago: American Library Association. This book is highly recommended. Although the format is based on the ACRL Information Literacy Standards, it provides samples of adaptable assessment materials that represent best practice in 27 higher education institutions in Australia, Canada and the United States.

8. Conclusion

Information literacy forms the basis for lifelong learning. It is common to all disciplines, to all learning environments, and to all levels of education.

(Iannuzzi et al., 2000, p. 2)

Information skills and lifelong learning

The Introduction to Chapter 1 states that if you are to succeed as a self-directed and lifelong learner you must not only have the skills that will enable you to make effective use of the information and communications technology that is available, you must also have the skills that will enable you to make effective use of the information that is available. Although you cannot be compelled to engage with this technology or with the vast range of information sources to which it offers such quick and easy access, it would be ill-advised if you ignored either, especially if you intend to make your career in education.

Put simply, if you choose to complete your course without learning how to access the information resources that your institution makes available, and without developing the skills that you will need in order to make effective use of that information, you will enter the employment market less well-informed and less skilled than many of those with whom you will be competing for jobs.

The level of skills competence that you will be expected to achieve will depend upon the course on which you are enrolled. At honours degree level, for example, you should be able to: critically evaluate the arguments of others; carry out analysis and enquiry to devise your own arguments; communicate information to specialist and non-specialist audiences; and manage your own learning (QAA, 2001, p. 8). That is, as an honours graduate you should have the skills, including the information and information technology skills, which will enable you to be a lifelong learner. The skills that are expected of students working at intermediate level, e.g. for a foundation degree or higher education diploma, are similar. (If you wish to examine the skills levels in more detail you can find them in the framework for higher education qualifications document on the QAA website. The URL for this document is included in the appropriate entry in the reference list at the end of the chapter.) Whatever your feelings about lifelong learning you should bear in mind that both the government and employers are committed to ensuring that 'everyone's skills and talents are developed throughout their lives' and that the level of skills competence expected of those who have received higher education is likely to be raised (DIUS, 2008).

Therefore it is in your interest to make the most of your time in higher education and this includes taking advantage of the opportunities that exist for you to develop your skills as well as your subject knowledge. In the case of information skills the two go together, since the more information literate that you become the more able you will be to critically engage with the theoretical content of your course and the better prepared to cope with your coursework.

Taking advantage of such opportunities does not mean that you must strive to become the highest achieving student on your course. Instead it means trying to do *your* best, and this requires you to be realistic about your ability to cope with information and information technology. It also means recognising that if you do not make the effort to acquire the skills that will enable you to get on top of information, then it will get on top of you. This is partly a matter of attitude and your attitude will, in turn, influence what you decide to do in order to make yourself more information literate and more technologically competent. Doing the bare minimum that is necessary in order to obtain a qualification is an option but it is not recommended as a coping strategy, and if you wish to survive in the Information Age you will need an effective coping strategy.

Having read through this book you may decide that one of your long-term aims should be to acquire and maintain an appropriate level of information literacy. In that case you must plan accordingly. (It should be pointed out that the alternative to having an aim is to be aimless, which means having no sense of direction or purpose. While this will spare you the bother of doing any planning, such an approach is unlikely to make you more information literate.)

Hopefully you will be persuaded that becoming more information literate is both a desirable and achievable aim. If so, it is up to you to decide how you intend to go about achieving it, since no one else can do the decision-making for you. However, having completed the self-assessment task in the previous chapter and having reflected upon the outcome, you should now have a much clearer idea of how information literate you are, and how much more information literate you will have to become in order to cope, as a student and a lifelong learner.

Sources of further information, help and advice

As with virtually any aspect of educational studies, there is such an increasing abundance of electronic sources of information, help and advice concerning information skills that it is only possible to include a very small sample of them here. Further, with a few exceptions, this sample deliberately excludes universities, since so many of them provide students with online help and advice on how to develop their information skills that a complete list of them would fill a book in itself. Therefore, if you find no mention of your own institution's information skills provision, it is because there was insufficient space to include it. There are, however, quick links to many relevant British (and foreign) university websites in some of sources that have been selected.

The extent to which any of the sources may be of practical use to you will, in part, depend upon how you perceive your information needs.

The International Information Literacy Resources Directory (InfoLitGlobal)

This database has been produced for Unesco by the International Federation of Library Associations and Institutions. It contains more than 1200 items, all of which are easy to browse by category and country, and to search by keyword. There are also quick links to 395 tutorials on how to use specific information resources, 119 information literacy websites, and numerous journals and other publications.

The database is divided into five main sections, as follows: Communication, Information Literacy Products for Users, Organizations, Publications, and Training the Trainers. In short, it is a veritable mine of information and it can be accessed at: www.infolitglobal.info/ .

Information Research: an international electronic journal

This is an open access, peer-reviewed and scholarly journal which publicises the results of information-related research across a wide-range of academic disciplines, including education. It was launched in1995 and is hosted by Lund University Libraries in Sweden. The current editor-in-chief is Professor Emeritus Tom Wilson from the University of Sheffield.

It is well indexed and can be quickly searched by author and subject. If you are interested in obtaining a sense of what its content is like you are advised to see the July 2003 issue. This contains an article by Sirje Virkus, at Manchester Metropolitan University, titled *Information literacy in Europe: a literature review.* Virkus discusses numerous developments across Europe and includes examples of initiatives in schools and universities, as well as various research projects. The main text and the reference list provide hyperlinks to many of the author's sources.

The journal can be accessed at: www.informationr.net/ir/

Online resources to support Big6 information skills

The Big6 is a very popular approach to teaching information and technology skills that has been developed in the United States and is mainly intended for use in schools. As its name suggests, it is based on six information skills. These are: task definition, information-seeking strategies, location and access, use of information, synthesis, and evaluation. The Online Resources site is formatted accordingly and it provides hyperlinks to more than 80 electronic resources that relate directly to the teaching of these skills.

While the resources are aimed at primary and secondary school teachers, rather than university students, you may find some of them of interest, especially if you intend to work in schools yourself.

The website can be accessed at: www.nb.wsd.wednet.edu/big6/big6_resources.htm .

Council of Australian University Librarians: Information Literacy Links

The council established an Information Literacy Working Group in 2003, to provide advice to its members. Their information literacy home page has links to 33 relevant Australian university websites, a list of publications, and nine pages of additional links to a wide range of organisations, resources and journal articles.

The Information Literacy Links website can be accessed at: www.caul.edu.au/info-literacy/links.html

The Information Literacy website and the Journal of Information Literacy

This website has been developed by information professionals from several organisations in the UK, including Eduserv, the Higher Education Academy, SCONUL, CILIP and the School Library Association. It provides links to over 40 online tutorials which have been developed by universities in the UK, Canada, the United States, Australia and New Zealand. In addition, it has a teaching resources page for staff working in schools and higher education institutions.

There is also a direct link to the international *Journal of Information Literacy*. This electronic journal, which was first published in 2007, is peer-reviewed and accepts papers on any topic that is related to the practical, technological or philosophical issues that arise from the attempt to promote information literacy.

The website can be accessed at: www.informationliteracy.org.uk/ and the journal at: www.informationliteracy.org.uk/JIL.aspx. (The URLs for the online tutorials can be found in the reference list at the end of the chapter.)

University of Sheffield Centre for Information Literacy Research

The centre, which is located within the university's Department of Information Studies, was launched in 2007 and its mission is to explore and develop the field of information literacy through research and related activities. The centre's website provides a brief description of its current research work and includes links to its growing publications list and its information literacy blogspot.

The department has also introduced a new MA in Information Literacy, further details of which can be downloaded from its website.

The website can be accessed at: www.sheffield.ac.uk/is/cilr

Open University Skills in Accessing, Finding and Reviewing Information (SAFARI)

SAFARI is an online tutorial programme that was launched by the Open University in 2002. It is divided into seven sections and each one covers a particular aspect of information skills. The programme also includes a series of topics for students to work through, many of which include reflective or practical tasks. Although non-OU students will be unable to access some of the resources that relate to these topics, if you are interested in a guided expedition through the information world, this is a good place to begin.

The website can be accessed at: www.open.ac.uk/safari/index.php

Manchester Metropolitan University Library and Leeds University Library: The Big Blue: final report

The Big Blue project was commissioned in 2001 to survey information skills training practice in FE and HE, and to make recommendations on how to ensure a coherent approach to the development of students' information skills. It was jointly managed by MMU and Leeds University and the *Final Report* was published in 2002.

While the report is primarily aimed at staff with responsibility for delivering information skills training, it is clearly set out in eight main sections (i.e. easy to read) and contains a great deal of information that is also likely to be of interest to students who would like to know more about the work that is being done on their behalf.

The report can be accessed at: www.library.mmu.ac.uk/bigblue/finalreport.html

Learning and Teaching Scotland Information Literacy Homepage

This is a very user-friendly website which is aimed at pupils aged 9 to18. It includes a wide range of information seeking and processing activities that have been designed according to pupils' age groups. Each has its own set of relevant information and study skills for pupils to learn and practise, and there are accompanying notes for teachers as well as parents.

In addition, there is a direct link on the site to the Scottish government's draft document titled *A national information literacy framework (Scotland)*.

The website can be accessed at: www.ltscotland.org.uk/informationliteracy/index.asp

A National Information Literacy Framework (Scotland)

As its title suggests, this draft document, which has been produced by Glasgow Caledonian University, discusses work that is being undertaken to develop a national and overarching framework of information literacy skills for all sectors of education in Scotland. The framework is seen as a key tool for ensuring that information literacy skills become embedded in the delivery of all curricula, from primary school to university level.

Although mainly aimed at library and information professionals, and learning and teaching organisations, the document is likely to be of interest to anyone with an interest in the teaching and learning of information skills.

The document can be accessed at: www.caledonian.ac.uk/ils/documents/DRAFT INFORMATIONLITERACYFRAMEWORK.lh.pdf

Summary of key points

You would be putting yourself at a considerable disadvantage if you were to complete your course without learning how to access the information sources that your institution makes available, and without developing the skills that you will need in order to make effective use of that information.

The more information literate that you become the more able you will be to engage critically with the theoretical content of your course and better prepared to cope with your coursework.

If you do not make the effort to acquire the skills that will enable you to get on top of information, then it will get on top of you.

It is up to you to decide how information literate you wish to become, and how you intend to go about achieving the level of information skills competence that you set for yourself.

References and further reading

Since most of these documents have already been discussed in the main body of the text or comments have been made about them in the reference lists in previous chapters, no further comments have been included here.

BIG6 (2005) *Online resources to support BIG6TM information skills.* [online] Available at: **www.nb.wsd.wednet.edu/big6/big6_resources.htm**

DIUS (2008) Consultation document *Higher education at work – high skills: high value.* London: Department for Innovation, Universities and Skills. [online] Available at: **www.dius.gov.uk/consultations/documents/Higher_Education_at_ Work.pdf**

Iannuzzi, P. et al. (2000) *Information literacy competency standards for higher education.* Chicago: American Library Association [online] Available at: http://www.ala.org/acrl/ilcomstan.html

Irving, C. and Crawford, J. (2007) *A national information literacy framework (Scotland).* Glasgow: Glasgow Caledonian University. [online] Available at: www.caledonian.ac.uk/ils/documents/DRAFTINFORMATIONLITERACY FRAMEWORK.lh.pdf

LTS (2007) *Information literacy home.* Glasgow: Learning and Teaching Scotland. [online] Available at: www.ltscotland.org.uk/informationliteracy/index.asp

MMU Library (2002) *The Big Blue: final report.* Manchester: Manchester Metropolitan University [online] Available at: www.library.mmu.ac.uk/bigblue/finalreport.html

Open University (2008) *Skills in accessing, finding & reviewing information.* Milton Keynes: The Open University. [online] Available at: www.open.ac.uk/safari/php_pages/about_safari.php

QAA (2001) *A framework for higher education qualifications in England, Wales and Northern Ireland.* Gloucester: Quality Assurance Agency for Higher Education. [online] Available at: www.qaa.ac.uk/academicinfrastructure/fheq/EWNI/default.asp

Index